MICHIGAN WATERFALLS

Text: Laurie Penrose
Maps: Bill T. Penrose
Photos: Ruth Penrose
Field Coordinator: Bill J. Penrose

THUNDER BAY
─── P R E S S ───

OTHER PENROSE GUIDEBOOKS

A Traveler's Guide to 116 Michigan Lighthouses
A Traveler's Guide to 100 Eastern Great Lakes Lighthouses
A Traveler's Guide to 116 Western Great Lakes Lighthouses

A Guide to 199 Michigan Waterfalls
Color Edition

Thunder Bay Press
4503 South M-76
West Branch, Michigan 48661

First Printing, May 1988
30th Anniversary Edition April 2018

ISBN 978-1-933272-64-1

Table of Contents

On May 30, 1934, at Negaunee, Michigan, Grace Anna Hubbert and Joseph Thomas Penrose were wed. Their abiding love has become our legacy, giving us the strength to test the waters of our own imagination. It is to each of them that we dedicate this book.

Front cover photos, clockwise from upper left:
Quartzite Falls (p. 66)
Judson Falls (p. 145)
Letherby Falls (p. 61)
Lower Montreal Falls (p. 105)

Back cover: Sable Falls (p. 7)

Acknowledgments

As with any endeavor of this magnitude, we couldn't have succeeded without the help of many wonderful people. We thank everyone who helped and supported us, especially:

Edmund Hedstrom, park manager, and Tom Proulx, park ranger, at Lake Gogebic State Park, for their assistance in Gogebic County.

Larry Harrington of the Crystal Falls DNR office for his assistance in the Iron County area.

Isabella Sullivan, with the Alger County Historical Society, for her information on the history of the Alger County area.

Grant Petersen, superintendent of the Pictured Rocks National Lakeshore, and his co-workers for their friendly help in the Pictured Rocks area.

Vern and Cora Killinger, West Branch, for their assistance with Spray Falls.

Jim, Todd and Kurt Penrose, Ishpeming, for their help in locating several of the falls in Marquette County.

Kelly Barry-Angeli of the Marquette County Chamber of Commerce for her help in the Marquette/Big Bay area.

Dan Plescher, Fort Wilkins State Park manager, for his assistance in the Baraga County area.

Bonny Kinnunen of the Baraga County Chamber of Commerce, one of the most informative and cooperative organizations in the U.P. We were very fortunate to find someone as friendly and as giving with time and knowledge as Bonny, and to her we extend special thanks.

Gary Barfknecht, for his belief in our project and his willingness to follow through on the arduous task of editing and publishing this volume.

Since our book was published, we have received many letters from readers and we would like to thank them for their additional information, with special thanks going to:

Gregg Bruff, Chief of Interpretation and Cultural Resources, Pictured Rocks National Lakeshore, for updated trail information on falls within that park.

Bonnie Peacock, USFS Watersmeet Ranger District, for supplying the information on Duppy Falls and others in the Watersmeet area.

Robert Batt, Wyoming, Michigan, for help with Au Train Falls and O-Kun-de-kun Falls, including beautiful pictures.

Todd Wayne Tucker, of Jackson, for helping with many falls but mainly for exploring the Dead River Falls area.

John Warning, St. Maries, Idaho, for information on many waterfalls.

Ben Larson, Trap Rock, for pointing the way to Fenners and 10-foot Falls.

William Eley, Waukegan, Illinois, for his help with many waterfalls throughout the Upper Peninsula.

Rick Kallioinen, Negaunee, for taking us to one of the most beautiful places in all of Michigan.

Tracy Barrett, Baraga County Tourist Association, who has been a great help for many years.

Jerry Keranen and his parents, Calumet, for their assistantce and support in the Calumet area.

Gary Penrose, Lansing, for his assistance on numerous trips, coming to the rescue in photographic emergencies, and making sure I didn't fall over a cliff.

Bill Penrose
West Branch, Michigan

Introduction

Michigan's Upper Peninsula is one of the most beautiful areas in the entire country. Throughout it all is the never-ending sound of waves upon sand, the roar of mighty rivers, and the shy laughter of tiny streams. The voice of the water never leaves you, and it is the underlying theme of this land.

The Upper Peninsula is a special place to our family. My great-grandparents left family and friends and journeyed from England to create a new life over the sea. From the tin mines of Cornwall to the iron mines of Michigan, the focus of our family had shifted. In the years following, many of us moved from the U.P. But no matter how far we go, the area always holds a special place in our hearts.

Some of my strongest memories are of walks in the Upper Peninsula in search of a forgotten spring or a run-down fenceline. No matter how enjoyable walking through the wilderness was, it was always better if you had a destination in mind. For this reason, many years ago we began to seek out the waterfalls of the U.P.

We wrote this book so that others could avoid many of the problems we encountered in our search for waterfalls. Incorrect maps, incomplete directions and unmarked trails were a constant source of irritation. But through hours of research and with the help of some very special people, we eventually found what we were looking for. It is with great pleasure we pass our findings along to you.

From falls you can peer at through your car window to those reachable only after an arduous hike deep into the interior of a forest, there are Michigan waterfalls for everyone. As with us, often your mood will determine what is most appealing, whether it be a long-forgotten pool beneath a gentle falls or the thunder of a river leaping into a gorge.

It's all there waiting for you.

Laurie Penrose
West Branch, Michigan

The Mackinac Bridge is considered by many to be the gateway to the Upper Penninsula.

Preface

We have made every effort to compose this guidebook in a manner that will make it an enjoyably useful tool. Following are some explanations of our terms and methods.

First, you may wonder why we have bothered to list some waterfalls only to subsequently advise you not to visit them. We have mentioned these falls because they are often included on other waterfall lists, even though in many cases they can't or shouldn't be visited for one or more reasons.

Directions: In the directions to most of the falls, the driving distance is noted in tenths of miles. These numbers may vary somewhat from vehicle to vehicle but should be fairly close.

When you hike to the falls, always take a compass. Though very small, it can suddenly become a large help in the midst of a thick forest. Also, always have a map on hand (U.S. Forest Service maps, a county map book or Michigan D.N.R. maps, for example) for the area you are visiting. Where there are no formal trails to the falls or where the route is complicated, we mark our way in with bright red ribbons, then remove them on the way out.

Private Property: We didn't knowingly visit falls that are on private property or where private property had to be crossed to get to them except in those instances when it was possible to obtain permission. We have noted the falls that are on private property, but we did not find out who the landowners are in most cases. If you wish to visit any of those falls, we urge you to find out locally who the landowner is and obtain permission. If this isn't possible, we recommend that you do not visit those falls.

Dams: Several waterfalls throughout the Upper Peninsula have had dams built on top of them, which in most cases eliminates the falls. In spite of this, most of these sites are still listed in waterfall directories, even though there are no visible waterfalls. Because of that, plus the fact that many are open to the public for fishing and boating, we have included mention of all dam sites that in the past have been called waterfalls as well as those we know are open to the public.

All dam sites are listed separately at the end of each chapter.

Nothing can compare to the isolated beauty of an Isle Royale sunrise.

UPPER TAHQUAMENON FALLS, p. 4

Chippewa and Luce Counties

More than 300 years of history, centered around Sault Ste. Marie, plus natural beauty such as the Hiawatha National Forest and the majestic Tahquamenon Falls, combine to make this one of the most interesting and beautiful areas of Michigan.

The first permanent European settlement in Michigan was at Sault Sainte Marie in 1668, and this historic community numbers among the oldest European settlements in the United States. During the 17th and 18th centuries, a lively mixture of people passed through and lived in the area as the flags of three different nations were raised over the city's rooftops. French fur traders of the 1600s were among the first to greet the native Americans, and a thriving trade developed. With the rise of British imperialism on the entire continent in the 1700s, England replaced France as the European power in the area. In 1828, 45 years after America won its independence, the last of the British finally left the area, but rugged fur traders were still the mainstay of the area's economy and activity.

In the mid-1800s everything changed. Industrialism hit Michigan with a vengeance. Copper and iron ore were discovered in the Upper Peninsula, and commerce there became increasingly important. However, getting the ore to eastern markets cheaply and efficiently via a Great Lakes water route was effectively blocked by the rapids of the St. Mary's River at Sault Ste. Marie. Powerful New York businessmen with interests in the iron and copper industry, however, formulated and carried out a then-remarkable plan to solve that problem, and in the process firmly anchored Sault Ste. Marie in the modern age.

In 1855 the first of the "Soo" locks, the engineering and construction marvel of the era, began dropping and raising vessels 21 feet between Lake Superior and Lake Huron. Today, it is one of the busiest lock systems in the world and also boasts the St. Lawrence Seaway's largest lock, which can service monstrous 1000-foot-long ore boats. From their opening, the Soo Locks have attracted millions of visitors, and just about everyone seems to find something fascinating in the wide variety of Great Lakes vessels and foreign ships that pass through the locks daily. One of the best spots to view the locks is right next to them from a beautiful park with lush landscaped lawns and flower beds nestled beneath shady trees. From there you are so close to the huge ships that it seems as though you can reach out and brush their steel sides with your hand.

Looming over the locks to the west is another engineering marvel, the International Bridge, a two-mile-long series of arches and trusses that spans the St. Mary's River to link the United States with Canada. Almost due south of the bridge is Lake Superior State University. Situated atop a hill, the campus occupies the site of Fort Brady, a U.S. Army post established in 1822.

As the St. Mary's River flows southeast from Sault Ste. Marie toward Lake Huron, it courses past dozens of islands, many of which are worth a visit. One short, scenic drive, for example, involves taking a ferry to Sugar Island, just east of Sault Ste. Marie. If you have time for a longer trip, take the ferry from DeTour Village to Drummond Island, the largest U.S. island on the Great Lakes, and spend the day exploring.

There are also many museums in the area, and two of particular interest are located in the Tahquamenon Falls area. Inside the Whitefish Point Lighthouse complex is the Great Lakes Shipwreck Museum, a collection of artifacts from ships that have sunk in the area. The displays not only viv-idly show the power of the Great Lakes, but also their hold over the men who sailed upon them. The Tahquamenon Logging Museum, north of Newberry on M-123, on the other hand, provides an opportunity to learn the history of the logging industry in Luce County. By looking at displays set up along the Tahquamenon River, you can easily imagine the frenzied activity of the early loggers as they worked this section of forest.

A mild January allows ore ship the *John G. Munson* to pass through the Soo Locks and out toward the open waters of Lake Superior.

St. Mary's Rapids

Early pre-locks photographs of the St. Mary's Rapids show a mass of white water churning roughly over the stones that line the riverbed, the foaming waves punctuated here and there with rocks rising up out of the water. The .75-mile-long rapids stretched the width of the river and, in the photos, appear as an unending blur that finally blended into the horizon upstream.

Unfortunately that grandeur was preserved only in photographs. Now just a narrow strip of the rapids flows between the Canadian and American locks at Sault Ste. Marie, and it is difficult to imagine their once-majestic scope.

The rapids that do remain are still impressive but hard to view. The best place to view them is from a Soo Locks tour boat or the Tower of History in downtown Sault Ste. Marie.

There used to be another, though less-well-known, rapids in the Sault area. If you take the car ferry from Sault Ste. Marie across the St. Mary's River to Sugar Island, you land on a small outer island separated from the main island by a wide channel. Black Point Rapids used to be located in this channel. We say "used to" because a solid earth causeway — built across the channel as an automobile route between the two islands — effectively cut off the water flow. So today, Black Point Rapids is just a calm, peaceful inlet off the river.

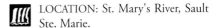 LOCATION: St. Mary's River, Sault Ste. Marie.

DIRECTIONS: From I-75, take either of the two business loops and follow the well-marked route to the Soo Locks. In downtown Sault Ste. Marie, turn right (east) onto Portage Ave. and go 0.3 miles to the Tower of History, 0.5 miles to Tour Boat Dock #2 or 1.7 miles to Tour Boat Dock #1.

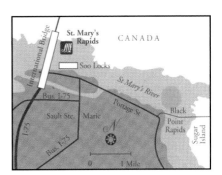

Lower Tahquamenon Falls

Just before its final 10-mile rush to Whitefish Bay, the wide Tahquamenon River splits around a center island and, at the same time, drops about 20 feet on both sides to form Lower Tahquamenon Falls. The deep, copper-colored water splashes over rough sections of large rocks and boulders strewn throughout the river, rejoins at the base of the island then slips away to the left. For a close-up look at both sections of the falls, take a rental rowboat to the island and walk the trails that circle its edge. You can also view them from lookout points on a high bluff about 100 feet in front of the parking area.

LOCATION: Tahquamenon River, 12.5 miles south of Paradise.

DIRECTIONS (Map, p. 4): On M-123 go west from Paradise approximately 12.5 miles to the Lower Tahquamenon Falls State Park, on the left.

This well-kept area, a small portion of Michigan's second-largest state park, is ideal for a picnic or even a day-long outing. Facilities include a park store, a playground, and picnic tables and grills set up in a grassy area surrounding the falls.

We also visited the falls in the winter. The road to the parking area was closed, so we had to walk about a mile down a large hill to reach the river. But the snow blanketing the forest created such silent, peaceful surroundings that it was a wonderful walk.

Upper Tahquamenon Falls

LOCATION: Tahquamenon River, 15½ miles southwest of Paradise.

DIRECTIONS: From M-123 go west from Paradise approximately 15.5 miles to signs on the left that point the way to the Upper Falls. The Lower Tahquamenon Falls are located 3 miles east on M-123.

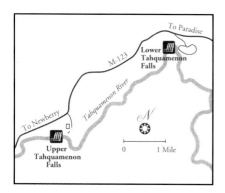

This is a falls you don't want to miss. Its enormity (it is the largest falls in Michigan) is spectacular. Golden water rushes over a 200-foot-wide slab of bedrock and drops with a mighty roar 50 feet to the river below. Mists rise up like sentinels and spread into the forest on both sides of the falls. The river here stretches through a deep canyon, and high walls of layered sandstone line the banks. These cliffs are painted with subtle reds and blues, which blend together as they reach the water.

The wide, paved trail that leads from the parking area to the falls forks as it nears the river. The left fork leads to downstream views of the falls; the right fork ends at a viewing area at the top of the falls. This fork eventually follows a ridge 75 feet above the river, and views along the route are sweeping, especially from the several turnoffs. The trail ends at a set of stairs that descend in several levels to a viewing platform at the very crest of the falls. This platform is constructed in such a way that you can view this mighty spectacle head-on.

Tahquamenon Falls is equally beautiful in the winter. Huge ice forms are created above and behind the sheet of falling water, and spires of ice reach up to meet the flow from the frozen river below. Icicles, created by water running from small streams over and between the rocks, decorate the canyon's stone walls. Mixed with the colored stone, the icicles take on a delicate blue tint, which highlights their sparkling beauty.

Facilities at this well-maintained state park include benches along the trails, drinking fountains and restrooms.

(Photo, p. *viii*)

Alger County

If you travel west across the Upper Peninsula, Alger is the first county with numerous waterfalls to visit. Many other natural wonders lie within the borders of this irregularly shaped parcel of land that borders Lake Superior in the north-central U.P. An added plus: large areas of state and federal land are open to the public throughout the county, including 70,000 acres administered by the National Park Service in the Pictured Rocks National Lakeshore.

That impressive scenic area stretches from Munising to Grand Marais and includes nearly

WAGNER FALLS (p. 17)

40 miles of breathtaking Lake Superior shoreline. You can experience an almost overwhelming solitude there, whether you sit beside cascading water, walk along the beaches in search of agates or watch the sun set across the vast expanse of Lake Superior. You can also absorb history. The Pictured Rocks area is the setting for many of the legends of Hiawatha, and as you stroll along the shore of Lake Superior, you are often following routes used by Ojibwa more than 100 years ago. Their paths are among miles of beautiful hiking trails that lead to waterfalls and other scenic areas throughout the park.

But the Pictured Rocks themselves — which stretch from just north of Munising for 15 miles northeast along Lake Superior — are the park's most prominent feature. You can glimpse the rocks from shore, but for the best views, take the Pictured Rocks Boat Tour that begins in Munising. A few miles from town, the rocky shoreline begins to rise until it forms huge, towering sandstone cliffs. The most unusual of these formations have been given names such as Miners Castle and Chapel Rock.

Past the Pictured Rocks are the Grand Sable Banks, huge cliffs of dark reddish-brown sand that fall steeply to meet the blue waters of Lake Superior. From these banks eastward toward Grand Marais is one of the best agate beaches in the Upper Peninsula.

Offshore from these beaches and stretching from AuTrain Point to the AuSable Point area is another unique park, an underwater diving preserve. The natural deep-water harbors of both Munising and Grand Marais have long attracted ships seeking shelter from raging Lake Superior storms. Many Great Lakes vessels, however, fell prey to their fury, and the lake bottom along all of Alger County's shoreline is littered with wrecks. The underwater preserve was established to allow diving while protecting those wrecks from pilfering. Several businesses in the area not only rent diving equipment, but also offer lessons and charters. Non-divers can view the hulls of several sunken ships from the shoreline. Just follow the beach from Hurricane River eastward until you reach AuSable Lighthouse. Along this stretch are the remains of many sunken ships, either a few feet under the water or sometimes partially buried in the beach itself.

The two cities that serve as the gateways to this unique area are also worth a visit. On the east is Grand Marais, a peaceful, picturesque village that rests on the shore of Lake Superior. On the west is Munising, which is bounded on the north by Lake Superior and enclosed on its other three sides by very high hills and ridges. That terrain is a natural location for waterfalls, and many are located either in the city itself or in the surrounding area.

Shipwreck remains between Hurricane River and Au Sable Lighthouse

Chipmunk Falls

According to local residents, not only do these falls run mainly only in the spring or after heavy rains, but also they are on private property and not open to the public.

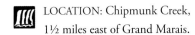 LOCATION: Chipmunk Creek, 1½ miles east of Grand Marais.

ALGER COUNTY WATERFALLS LOCATED WITHIN THE PICTURED ROCKS NATIONAL LAKESHORE: Sable Falls, Spray Falls, Chapel Falls, Unnamed Falls, Mosquito Falls, Bridal Veil Falls, Miners Falls, Munising Falls, Miners Beach Falls, Unnamed Falls near Miners Beach, and Hurricane River Falls

Note: Because a network of converging trails crosses the Pictured Rocks National Lakeshore, we advise that you pick up a trail map from one of the two visitors centers located near both park entrances.

Sable Falls

Located just west of Grand Marais, Sable Falls (photo, back cover) marks the east border of the Pictured Rocks National Lakeshore. The falls drops through a deep valley the river has carved into the surrounding sand and heavy underlying bedrock, and high sand cliffs border the flow on both sides. Though relatively small, Sable Falls is nevertheless dramatic as it courses over large boulders strewn in its path.

The quarter-mile path to the falls from a parking lot about a mile west of Grand Marais is smooth, wide and very easy going. At the falls itself, an extensive stairway system drops to another path, to the right of the river, which leads to one of the best agate beaches in Michigan.

An alternate route (and a good afternoon excursion) is to park in the Grand Marais Municipal parking lot and walk west down the beach about a mile, until you reach the mouth of Sable Creek. From there, you can walk less than a quarter of a mile to the falls, or continue down the shore along the Grand Sable Banks, a majestic sight you won't want to miss. To get closest to the banks, drive west on H-58 to Grand Sable Lake, with opportunities for swimming and fishing where the road curves around the huge dunes that brush up against the lake's north shore. For a better view of the dunes, continue along H-58 to the Log Slide turnoff, 7.5 miles west of Grand Marais.

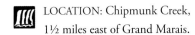 LOCATION: Sable Creek 1½ miles west of Grand Marais.

DIRECTIONS: Go west out of Grand Marais on H-58 for about one mile to a parking lot, on the right, and the start of the trail to Sable Falls.

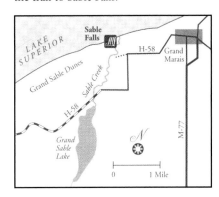

Hurricane River Falls and Rapids

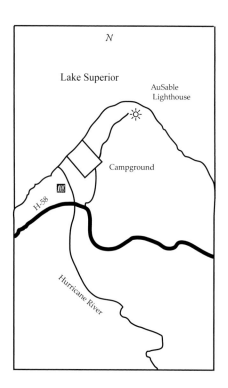

LOCATION: Hurricane River, at the Hurricane River Campground.

DIRECTIONS: Drive north on H-58 to the Hurricane River Campground, in the Pictured Rocks National Lakeshore, about 39 miles northeast of Munising or about 13 miles west of Grand Marais. As you enter the campground, park near the river and walk to the lake. You will see the rapids at the mouth of the river and the waterfall is a very short distance upstream, just above the footbridge.

The Hurricane River empties into Lake Superior at a beautiful stretch of shoreline along the Pictured Rocks National Lakeshore. From the parking area, take the trail down to the lakeshore, which leads past a small set of stairs down to the sandy beach. At the mouth of the river, its copper-colored currents make interesting shapes in the sand and gravel, while the twisted limbs of birches line the banks of the river. The last 100 yds. of the river is a quick-running series of rapids as the water rushes around the black and brown stone and past mossy trunks, dropping about 5 ft. on the last leg of its journey to Lake Superior. A pretty footbridge spans the river here, inviting visitors to investigate the opposite bank.

About 200 yds. upstream, the water drifts over a ledge of black stone, falling in sharp twists over boulders and fallen trees before creating a beautiful pool below. Pillows of foam skate across the surface of the pool before being sucked downstream and the waiting rapids beyond.

The Hurricane River is the perfect spot for a family getaway. It offers not only the falls and rapids, but a beautiful expanse of Lake Superior shoreline, where the gold sand is dotted here and there with rounded boulders protruding from the water's surface. There is a trail to the AuSable Lighthouse, one of Michigan's most beautiful beacons, and rangers lead weekly hikes and give talks on the history of the area. If you are interested in lighthouses and their history, we recommend *A Traveler's Guide to 116 Michigan Lighthouses*, also written by our family.

Spray Falls

The isolation and powerful beauty of this falls make it one of the most enjoyable in the area. Spray Creek — a small stream that winds its way through the birches, hemlocks and mountain ash of the surrounding forest — finally bursts free of its confines and dramatically plunges nearly 70 feet directly into the sparkling blue waters of Lake Superior.

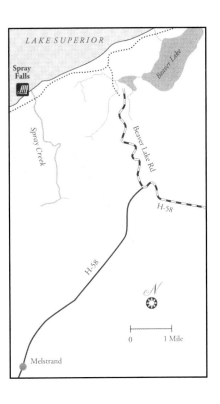

LOCATION: Spray Creek, 6½ miles north of Melstrand.

DIRECTIONS: Drive approximately 5 miles east of Melstrand on H-58 to Beaver Lake Rd. Turn left (north) onto Beaver Lake Rd. and go approximately 3 miles to a parking area on the left (before you reach Little Beaver Campground.) It is about a 3-mile walk to Spray Falls from this parking area. The trail to Spray Falls is part of a network of trails in the Pictured Rocks National Lakeshore, and since there are several converging trails in the area, we advise that you pick up a trail map from one of the two visitors centers located near both park entrances.

From the parking area, take the left loop of the White Pine Trail, then cross the creek at the next junction. After 1.5 miles this connector trail meets the Lakeshore Trail, which runs the length of the national lakeshore along the rim of the Pictured Rocks and offers some spectacular views of the multicolored cliffs and the deep blue-greens of the lake. Turn left and walk west along the Lakeshore Trail for about 2 miles to Spray Falls. There are no signs announcing it, so when you approach the area keep alert for the sounds of the falls splashing into the lake far below. A wooden bridge spans Spray Creek, but since the falls faces Lake Superior, you must view it from any area of the trail that extends farther out into the lake before the trail reaches the small stream.

A note of caution: do not leave the trail in this area, as the rock has been undercut in many places along the shoreline and can be very unstable.

SPRAY FALLS

Bridal Veil Falls
Jasper Falls

LOCATION: 8 miles northeast of Munising.

DIRECTIONS: To get to Miners Castle, go east on H-58 from Munising approximately 4.5 miles to Miners Castle Road. Turn north onto Miners Castle Road and go about 5 miles to its end. *(see map, pg. 15)*

This falls is usually only a spring runner, but we were lucky enough to see it after a heavy summer rainfall.

Silvery white tendrils of water fan out over the cliffs of the Pictured Rocks and slide 100 feet down to meet the world's largest freshwater lake. And as they run down the smooth, multicolored stone, they form the reason for the fall's name — an outline remindful of a bride's veil.

For the easiest, though distant, views of this falls, look northeast from the observation platform high atop the rock formation called Miners Castle. Avid hikers can get closer by walking approximately two miles along the Lakeshore Trail from Miners Castle. We do not recommend this hike for the average tourist, however, because of the dangerous cliffs in the area.

The best way to view the falls is to take the boat tour out of Munising. On that tour, you will also be able to view Jasper Falls, a delicate stream which dances over the rocky shelf for three or four feet before plunging into Lake Superior. Jasper Falls is the first waterfall you will see on the boat trip, and can only be viewed from the lake.

JASPER FALLS

BRIDAL VEIL FALLS

Chapel Falls

You can get to both Chapel and Mosquito Falls from the same parking area, and if you have time, you should visit both. Chapel Falls, which is more popular, is dramatic, whereas Mosquito Falls is secluded and personal.

The 1.5-mile trail to Chapel Falls, though steep at times, is actually more like a road. It is very wide, and well-maintained. As you approach the river, the path skirts a ridge, and through the trees you can glimpse the sweeping vista of rolling hills that surround Chapel Lake far below.

As you hike to the falls, take advantage of two scenic overlooks at the end of short side trails. The first overlooks Chapel Lake; the second provides a beautiful view of the falls from the west side.

For a closer look at the falls you must cross Section 34 Creek, which is easily accomplished on a small bridge built by the park service. Once across, a 100-yard-long foot trail leads to a clearing on a bluff (a perfect spot for a picnic) with a riveting view of the falls and tree-covered canyon. Framed by pine boughs, white spray hurls itself over the cliff, passes briefly over the black rock, then gathers its forces to rush through an opening in the trees. This falls is aptly named, for the panorama inspires a powerful sense of serenity.

If you like to hike, you can continue from the falls on a trail that circles Chapel Lake then heads toward Lake Superior. Although we didn't try it, that day-long walk is both beautiful and popular, according to park service personnel.

LOCATION: Section 34 Creek, 5½ miles north of Melstrand.

DIRECTIONS: From H-58 just north of Melstrand, turn left onto a gravel road marked by a Chapel Falls sign and continue to follow the signs about 6 miles to the Chapel Falls parking area. The trail to Chapel Falls heads east from the parking area.

CHAPEL FALLS

MOUTH OF CHAPEL CREEK

UNNAMED FALLS ON CHAPEL CREEK

Unnamed Falls

LOCATION: Chapel Creek, 4 miles northwest of Melstrand.

DIRECTIONS: From H-58 just north of Melstrand turn left onto a gravel road marked by a Chapel Falls sign and continue to follow the signs about 6 miles to the Chapel Falls parking area. As you approach the parking lot you will cross a small stream. After parking your vehicle, walk back down the road, cross the stream, then turn right and follow the stream as noted in the text.

Just south of the Chapel Falls parking area, a small stream slips beneath the roadway and flows west to Chapel Creek and an unnamed falls. The absence of a well-worn trail to the falls makes for rough going over a few spots and also sets up the possibility of getting lost. But if you stay close to the flowing water, you shouldn't have a problem. As you follow its left bank, the small creek makes several one-foot drops over smooth stone shelves. The banks rise until, about 100 yards from the road, you look down on the stream's junction with Chapel Creek from a height of about 12 feet.

From the junction go left, up Chapel Creek, about 50 yards to the falls. You will approach the falls on a high cliff with steep sides to the canyon below, so use extreme care. The falls themselves consist of a 200-foot-long series of drops, the highest falling about 30 feet into the steep canyon below. From the top of the ridge, you can only glimpse this falls in sections.

To get a better view, you would have to walk in the canyon itself, that is, remain on the banks of both the unnamed creek and Chapel Creek. That would not be easy, however. The banks of both streams are sometimes steep, which would require some difficult maneuvering.

Alger County

Mosquito Falls

Though somewhat small and unimposing, Mosquito Falls is very accessible and charming in a quaint way. The Mosquito River here slides, then cascades over layers and shelves of black rock, leaving small pools in its wake. Visitors are asked to stay on the trail, due to the delicate beauty of the fragile vegetation.

Chapel Falls is located only about 2½ miles from Mosquito Falls, and if you have time, you should visit both.

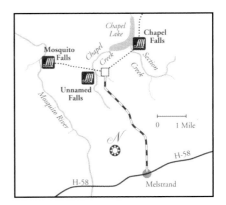

MOSQUITO FALLS

LOCATION: Mosquito River, 5 miles northwest of Melstrand.

DIRECTIONS: From H-58 just north of Melstrand turn left onto a gravel road marked by a Chapel Falls sign and continue to follow the signs about 6 miles to the Chapel Falls parking area. A newly constructed trail directly to Mosquito Falls heads west from the parking area and is a well-marked, 1.3-mile route. You can return along the same trail or follow a much longer loop out to Lake Superior and back to the parking area.

2 Miners Beach Area Falls

LOCATION: Miners Beach, 6 miles northeast of Munising.

DIRECTIONS: On H-58 drive east from Munising approximately 4.5 miles to Miners Castle Road and go about 5 miles to Miners Beach Road. Turn right and follow this road for 1 mile to its end. Turn right and go .2 mile where the road will end in the Lakeshore Trail Parking Area. Take the Mosquito Falls trail, which begins at the parking area, and follow it about 300 yards to a trail on the left, where the rocks rise out of the ground. Follow this trail beside the bluff for about 150 yards to the falls. To visit the falls on Miners Beach, drive back for .4 mile (passing Miners Beach Road) to the Miners Beach Parking Area. Park and walk the beach east about .3 mile to its end. The falls will be on your right.

A wide path takes you to the grotto which is home to the Unnamed Falls near Miner's Beach. As you approach the falls, the rock bluff overhead becomes undercut, and the small creek falls away from the layered stone of the bluff. Only a few hundred yards from the shoreline, the falls is still a secluded and quiet example of the beauty that is around every corner of the National Lakeshore. Even though it is in close proximity to the shoreline, we recommend taking the trail back to the parking area and driving down to Miner's Beach to visit the second falls in this area, as the terrain from this falls to the next can be very damp and thickly overgrown.

The beach in this area is beautiful, with its backdrop of deep greens as the forest reaches out towards Lake Superior. As you follow the beach to the right, small pockets of rock peek out from the golden sand, gradually turning a beach into a rocky coastline. As you reach the falls, a small creek escapes from the darkness of the forest, creating its own dark path as it meanders across the layers of rock and out into the lake. It drops in several sections for a total of about 9 feet.

UNNAMED FALLS, MINERS BEACH

Miners Falls

A clearly marked, wide, smooth path — which curves for half a mile through tall, stately hardwoods — leads to one of the most popular waterfalls in the Pictured Rocks National Lakeshore. At the end of the route, a short trail to the left ends at a viewing platform. For a closer look, you can descend an extensive stairway, which becomes a fairly strenuous climb as you leave.

The Miners River here spills out of the forest, then drops 30 to 40 feet in a forceful stream of white spray. Behind the flow, a small hollow has formed in the face of the cliff. The force of the water has worn other round holes in the bedrock at the base of the falls to create some interesting patterns and compositions in the stone's surface.

When you visit Miners Falls, we highly recommend a side trip to Miners Castle, north of the falls. Although the highest parts of the rocky tower have fallen, you still get a breathtaking view of the Pictured Rocks and the blue-green waters of Lake Superior directly below. RV parking is available there as well as restrooms (open during the summer months) with facilities for the handicapped.

 LOCATION: Miners River, 6 miles northeast of Munising.

DIRECTIONS: On H-58 drive east from Munising approximately 4.5 miles to Miners Castle Road and go about 3.5 miles to a road marked by a "Miners Falls" sign. Turn right (east) and follow this road to the Miners Falls parking area and the start of the trail to the falls.

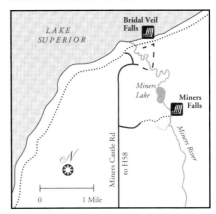

Munising Falls

Just inside the eastern limits of the city of Munising, a paved path through the woods that lines Munising Creek leads to the most visited falls in Alger County.

For many years the path continued up and along the side of the cliff, so that you were actually able to walk behind the waterfall. But cave-ins in 1995 took out a section of the path and made the area near the falls too hazardous. The trail behind the falls has been blocked off and can no longer be used.

The five-minute walk from the Munising Falls Interpretive Center ends at a platform and some excellent views of the "pride of Munising." The falls drops a sheer 40-50 feet into a canyon of multicolored rocks. Rosy hues mix with earth

LOCATION: Munising.

DIRECTIONS: From M-28 where it makes a 90-degree turn in Munising, go east on M-58 (Munising Ave.) about 1¼miles to Washington St., on the left. Turn left (north) onto Washington and go a little more than ½ mile to where it bears right, at a hospital. The Munising Falls parking area is located across the street from the hospital. (You can, in fact, use the hospital signs along the route to direct you to the falls.)   *(see map. pg. 16)*

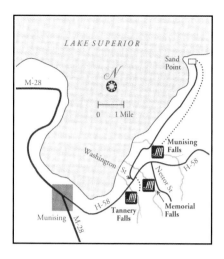

browns and golds to frame the water with color.

Munising Falls is just as beautiful in the winter. The motion of its cascades is frozen like a stop-action picture, with a huge, apparently solid pillar of ice that stretches the entire height of the falls. But if you move close enough you can catch a glimpse of water still falling beneath the frozen shell. Rarely will you get the chance to see such a beautiful, majestic sight with so little effort. The path to the falls is kept clear, and to our surprise even the visitors center restrooms were open during our winter visit.

During the summer the building is alive with activity, including interpretive programs. Maps of the Pictured Rocks National Lakeshore are displayed, and pleasant, informative park personnel can answer any questions you might have about the area. There's plenty of room for RVs in the parking lot, and a wheelchair is available at the front desk.

Memorial Falls

LOCATION: Unnamed creek, Munising.

DIRECTIONS: From M-28 where it makes a 90-degree turn in Munising, go east on H-58 (Munising Ave.) about 1½ miles to Nestor St., on the right. Turn right (south) onto Nestor and go about a block to signs, on the right, that mark the trails to Memorial Falls.

Several paths through this beautiful natural area lead to the falls. Because of the fragile nature of the area, please stay on the existing trails. Also, since you approach Memorial Falls from the top of the canyon, use extreme care.

A short, easy trail through a beautiful natural setting leads to the edge of a deep canyon where a 3-foot-wide stream plunges over the lip, hits a rock ledge, then continues its 30-foot drop to the sandy floor below. Tall sandstone walls, which extend downstream and out of sight, seem to stand guard over this delicate falls. The rock walls on both sides of the stream are deeply undercut, even behind the falls itself, which creates an area of deep shadows behind strands of sparkling water. Tall pines and hardwoods blanket the top of the rock ridges to the very edge, where their roots snake down the surface of the rock.

A wooden walkway leads over the top of the cliff near the falls and then down to the floor of the small canyon close to the base of the falls.

Memorial Falls is a relatively new addition to the list of Alger County falls. It has been around for thousands of years, of course, but was not open to the public until 1987. At that time it became part of a public nature preserve opened by the Michigan Nature Association, which had purchased land surrounding this falls as well as nearby Tannery Falls.

MUNISING FALLS (pg. 15)

Tannery Falls
(also called Rudy M. Olson Memorial Falls)

LOCATION: Tannery Creek, Munising.

DIRECTIONS: From M-28 where it makes a 90-degree turn in Munising, go east on H-58 (Munising Ave.) about 1¼ miles to the intersection with Washington St., on the left. Park on Washington and walk back across H-58 to the trail, marked with a sign, to the falls.

The trail on the south side of the river is easy walking on high ground all the way to the falls.

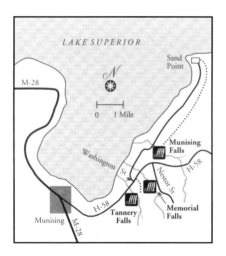

The walk to Tannery Falls (renamed Rudy M. Olson Memorial Falls) is as beautiful as the falls themselves. The layered patterns in the surrounding soft sandstone are exquisite, and the trail affords a close-up view of their golden rose colors. As the trail approaches the falls, the canyon walls rise upward, curve toward the center and extend slightly over the trail. A mound of debris — dirt and stones that have fallen from the sides of the cliff — have piled up to fill a portion of the bowl in front of the falls. Narrow Tannery Creek flows over the side of the sandstone layers, fans out across the mossy steps, then falls 40 feet directly to the floor of the canyon below. There, the white tendrils of water rejoin, and the stream cuts to the right and grazes the sandstone wall as it continues on its course. Tannery Falls has always been a beautiful falls but, under private ownership, was closed to the public for many years. Thanks to the Michigan Nature Association — which purchased the land surrounding Tannery Falls and created a public nature preserve that also includes nearby Memorial Falls — it is open to the public once again.

ALGER FALLS (opposite page)

Horseshoe Falls

Located inside the city limits of Munising, Horseshoe Falls is so accessible that it shouldn't be missed. An added attraction is some entertainment for children, who may become bored on long hikes to some of the other falls in the area.

Horseshoe Falls is privately owned, and you have to pass through a small gift shop, plus pay a small fee to view them. Outside the gift shop, a fence encloses a trout pond, where the kids (or you) can feed the fish. A paved walkway meanders through a small botanical garden, and a trail to the right leads less than 100 feet to the falls.

The falls itself is small, with a stream falling about 40 feet over the lip of a bowl. The water then bubbles around a few boulders and continues on its way under some small foot bridges. A hollow, which cuts deeply into the face of the cliff, originally gave the falls a very distinct horseshoe shape. But with the passing of time, falling rocks and earth have changed the contour of the rock walls, and the original shape is no longer well-defined.

 LOCATION: Stutts Creek, Munising.

DIRECTIONS: From M-28 near Munising's southern limits (about ½ mile north of Alger Falls), turn east onto Prospect St. and go approximately 2 blocks to Bell Ave. Turn left (north) onto Bell and go approximately a block to the Horseshoe Falls parking area and gift shop, on the right.

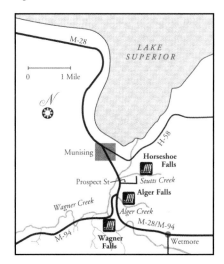

Alger Falls

Just a few yards from M-28, a small outcropping of rocks emerges from the surrounding hillside, and water spills over them in a series of cascades. Despite its proximity to the highway, the serenity of this falls prevails as it drops through a small, almost overlooked valley.

It couldn't be any easier to view Alger Falls. Just pull your vehicle off the highway and study its simple beauty through the window if you like. However, for more intimate views or better camera angles, walk about 30 feet closer to the river.

LOCATION: Alger Creek, one mile south of Munising.

DIRECTIONS: From Munising go south on M-28 approximately one mile to where M-94 branches off to the right (west). Alger Falls is on the left (east) side of M-28 at this point.

Wagner Falls

LOCATION: Wagner Creek, 1½ miles south of Munising.

DIRECTIONS: From Munising go south on M-28 approximately one mile to where M-94 branches off to the right (west). Turn right (west) onto M-94 and go approximately ½ mile to a small roadside area (marked by a Wagner Falls sign) on the left (south).

The path to the falls is only about 300 yards long, and an improved trail makes hiking through the swampy area much easier. After that, wooden walkways cover the muddy sections of the trail. We visited on a rainy afternoon, and the walkways were slippery. But the path quickly climbed, then ran through a forest of translucent greens and golden fall colors. (see map, pg. 19)

A substantial volume of water confined to a relatively small space makes Wagner Falls a roaring, powerful example of one of Michigan's small waterfalls. The falls is narrow but deep, and the water slides over several heavy rock ledges. Large rocks divide the stream, and several fallen trees bridge the sides of the falls.

Wagner Falls, located within easy driving distance of Alger Falls, was donated to the people of the State of Michigan by the Michigan Division of the Women's Farm and Garden Association Inc.

WAGNER FALLS

Upper Wagner Falls

If you're a little more adventurous and want to explore beyond the viewing platform, two more falls await further upstream. On the wooden walkway, just before reaching the stairs, you'll see a small stream passing beneath the walkway. Just beyond this to the right, a narrow path leads up through the forest along the ridge above the river. The path is steep in spots, and can be slippery in wet weather. The banks of the river are very steep, and hikers must use caution even in excellent weather. As you follow the narrow trail through the thick pine forest, about 300 ft. upstream you can glimpse the wall of foamy white cascading beyond the delicate pine branches. The river drops about 25 ft. here in two stages. The banks are a little too steep to leave the relative safety of the trail, but you can see the falls between the trees as it noisily rushes down the rocky banks.

Another falls awaits about 150 ft. upstream. This waterfall drops about 15 ft. as the river contracts to half its width, racing over the brown stone which forms its banks. It's much easier to reach the riverbank here, and you can get a good view of the falls. After its drop, the river rests a bit, meandering around the smaller rocks in midstream, framed by the fallen trees stretching over its width, before continuing its race to Lake Superior.

UPPER WAGNER FALLS

Scott Falls

LOCATION: 8 miles northwest of Munising.

DIRECTIONS: Scott Falls is located on the south side of M-28 just east of H.J. Rathfoot State Roadside Park, approximately 2 miles east of AuTrain.

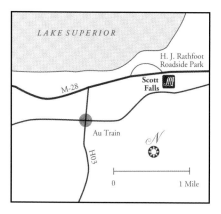

Scott Falls is close enough to M-28 to view from your car. However, it is such a charming falls, we suggest that you get close enough to feel the water with your hands.

A medium-size stream of water drops about 10 feet directly into a small pool lined with sand and small pebbles. The rock shelf behind the stream has been hollowed out, so it is possible to walk behind the falls and hold out your hand to catch the strong rush of water.

Scott Falls is not only a fun, popular break for automobile travelers, but also can be a stopover for snowmobilers. In the winter its heavy stream forms a beautiful column of ice. The cave behind the frozen pillar is covered with an icy carpet, and large icicles decorate the walls.

SCOTT FALLS

Alger County

Silver Bell Falls

Humbly beginning from tiny Nelson Creek, Silver Bell Falls (sometimes called Silver Falls) remains small but drops about 30 feet over the dark, layered side of a steep cliff in the middle of the woods. As the water falls down the side of the soft mossy wall, it widens to about 10 feet. Viewed from either side, the falls is beautiful in its simplicity. It is especially nice in the spring or after a heavy rain, when the creek, and thus the falls, swells in size.

Before or after your visit to Silver Bell Falls, we recommend a trip to Rock River Falls. The two are very close together and are good comparisons of the diversity of Michigan waterfalls.

LOCATION: Nelson Creek, 7½ miles northwest of Chatham.

DIRECTIONS: From M-94 where it makes a 90-degree bend in Chatham, turn north onto Rock River Rd. Go 3.5 miles, cross the Rock River, then go another 0.1 miles to USFS-2276. This road is narrow and rocky but in good condition. Turn left (west) onto 2276 and go approximately 3.6 miles to where it jogs sharply left. Continue straight for 0.9 miles to an iron gate that crosses the road.

The mile walk to the falls begins at that gate. After 10 minutes of walking, the road forks; follow the right fork straight ahead, past a small parking area on the right to where the road turns into a trail. Continue straight ahead on this trail, over a culvert at about 50 yards, to the falls, about 50 feet farther, on the right.

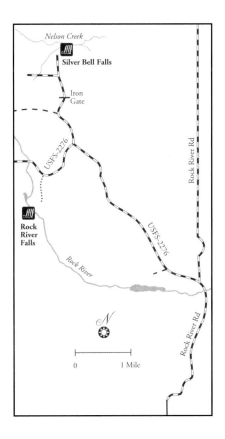

Rock River Falls

A 20-foot drop in the Rock River near Chatham has created one of the most beautiful, secluded falls in Alger County. And though the falls are still remote, extensive work done by the U.S. Forest Service has made it much easier to reach them than in the past.

As we traveled the path to the falls, we noticed a large, abandoned sled at the side of the trail. When we got closer, we could see that it was an old logging sled, with trees growing through it that were at least 20 years old. It was strange to see a remnant of civilization in such a remote location, but it reminded us that we were not the first to travel this way, nor would we be the last.

After a half-hour walk through thick, beautiful woods, we reached the river about 30 yards above the falls. The river here

LOCATION: Rock River, 5 miles northwest of Chatham.

DIRECTIONS: From M-94 where it makes a 90-degree bend in Chatham, turn north onto Rock River Rd. Go 3.5 miles, cross the Rock River, then go another 0.1 mile to USFS-2276. This road is narrow and rocky but in good condition. Turn left (west) onto 2276 and go approximately 4.3 miles (jogging sharply left at 3.6 miles) to a small parking area on the left marked by a sign pointing the way to the trail to Rock River Falls. The ¾-mile-long path is mostly downhill, and the ground becomes wet as you reach the bottom.

ROCK RIVER FALLS

is divided into two streams by a dry rock area, which traps the autumn leaves. The water slides out of the woods under fallen trees and past rocky banks, then drops about 20 feet down the side of a rock ledge. The water catches on the steps of the ledge, creating progressively smaller streams, which form feathery trails from top to bottom. The best view of the falls comes from directly in front of it.

At the base of the falls is a large, dark and apparently still pool. Those adventurous enough to wade, however, will discover that the hidden current of the river pulls through it.

While in the area we met a native who recommended a cross-country ski trip from Rumely (a small town four miles southwest of the falls) to the valley that surrounds the river and falls. The man, a forest-service employee, said it is a particularly beautiful trip because ice caves — walls of ice created when water seeps out of the side of the rock and freezes — line the valley in the winter.

Before or after your visit to Rock River Falls, we recommend a trip to Silver Bell Falls. The two are very close together and are good comparisons of the diversity of Michigan waterfalls.

Au Train Falls

LOCATION: Au Train River, 10 miles southwest of Munising.

DIRECTIONS: From the junction of M-28/M-94 south of Munising, go west on M-94 approximately 12.5 miles to the village of Forest Lake. Approximately ¼ mile west of town, turn right (north) onto H03, the first road past the Au Train River. On H03, cross the railroad tracks, then turn right (east) onto the first gravel road (marked with an "Au Train Falls" sign). The parking area is at the end of this road, and the trail to the falls starts at the iron gate.

On the left as you descend to the falls from the parking area, small trickles of water continuously run over and down rock walls, which are covered by a thick layer of moss in some areas. This unusual smooth cliff was carved out of the heavy stone shelf by the local power company as they cut the short but steep access road to the falls.

At the bottom, as you turn and look back up, you realize that the trees on the right side of the path are hiding something. The river sweeps out of the forest in a thin layer of sparkling water that carpets smooth rock shelves.

A bridge, also built by the power company, effectively breaks the panorama of the falls in half. Even so, the view is sweeping. The level of the 60-foot-wide river drops in a series of short cascades and tumbling water, then slides under the steel bridge.

Below the bridge, the river runs much the same, with the addition of a few small natural fishing and wading pools. The pools look inviting, but be sure of your footing if you wade. The shallow water and smooth rocks make for ideal growth conditions for slippery moss and algae.

There is an equally impressive falls farther upstream about a tenth of a mile from the parking area, at the point where the aquaduct crosses the river.

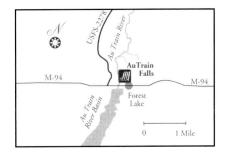

Laughing Whitefish Falls

Laughing Whitefish Falls' spectacular 100-foot drop, plus its deep gorge and layered limestone walls make it one of the most beautiful in Alger County. As you gaze up from its base at the huge wall of sparkling, shimmering rock, it's hard to believe that it all comes from just one small stream.

No large rushes of water pour over the face of the rock. The water's movement is traced only by a general dampness in shaded areas and a blinding brilliance in the sunlit sections. (The reflections off the water make it difficult to take photographs when the sun is directly overhead, which unfortunately is when the falls is most spectacular.) The stream continues along the layered limestone and catches in a small pool, and only the twinkling of the water betrays its movement as it runs its course unaffected by the falls it has just left behind.

The 20-minute walk to the falls is mostly downhill through a lovely hardwood forest. The trail begins as a well-kept woodchip-covered path through a meadow filled with berry bushes and tall grasses. Wildflowers peek out through the clumps of bushes and young trees until the trail cuts through a thickly wooded area about a half mile to an extensive flight of stairs. The falls doesn't announce itself with a roar of water or any sudden, sweeping vistas, and it comes as almost a surprise when you reach the top of the stairs.

As you climb or descend the stairs, you can rub your hands along the shallow depressions and caves that line the rim of the canyon. Also from the stairs you can see small streams as they wind their way through the undergrowth to the base of the falls.

 LOCATION: Laughing Whitefish River, 2½ miles northeast of Sundell.

DIRECTIONS: From M-94 in Sundell, turn north onto Dorsey Rd. (at a Michigan scenic-site sign) and go approximately 2 miles to a gravel road (also marked with a scenic-site sign). Turn right (east) and follow this road approximately ½ mile to the Laughing Whitefish Falls parking area.

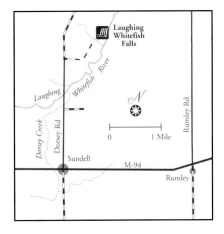

Whitefish Falls

LOCATION: Whitefish River, 5 miles northwest of Trenary.

DIRECTIONS: From the intersection of M-67 and US-41 (approximately ¾ mile west of Trenary on M-67 and about 18 miles north of Rapid River on US-41), go north on US-41 approximately 3.5 miles and turn left onto the first gravel road past Diffin Rd., on the left. This fairly wide, well-maintained trail road loops back to US-41 about ¼ mile north, so you don't have to turn your vehicle around to leave. As you reach the point where the loop is farthest from US-41, you will be able to hear the river. Park in this area, walk down the bank to the river, and head upstream.

Whitefish Falls is actually a series of three drops spaced at about 50-yard intervals. The first falls comes into distant view early in the short walk to them. As you get closer you see that across the entire width of the river the water drops about four feet and becomes copper-colored as it rushes over the bedrock slabs. Farther upstream the second and third falls, each with a drop of about a foot, form twin copper bands that span the river.

The trail to the falls is only about 150 yards long, but it is a lovely walk along the banks of a beautiful river. Huge cedars and hardwoods bend out over the water from the large limestone slabs that border both sides. The stone "carpet" provides a very easy path to follow, and it also is a good place to sit and soak your feet in the swift current.

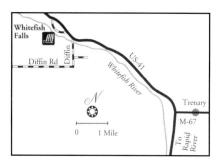

WHITEFISH FALLS

Alger County

Marquette County

Marquette County, Michigan's largest in land area, is truly a vacationer's paradise. Its borders enclose more lakes, 835, than any other Michigan county, and its more than 1,000,000 acres of land is networked with hundreds of miles of snowmobile, hiking and cross country ski trails. Downhill skiers, too, have many areas to choose from, and skiers and non-skiers alike will enjoy a visit to the National Ski Hall of Fame in Ishpeming.

The city of Marquette, home of Northern Michigan University, is the center of the county's activity. The iron ore industry first opened up this area, and you can still watch ore being loaded onto huge Great Lakes ships at the world's first pocket ore dock. But Marquette now has many other industries plus a beautifully restored downtown business district built along the hillsides bordering Lake Superior.

The lake, in fact, has become the focal point of the city, and one of the most beautiful of the many attractions lining its shore is Presque Isle Park. A paved roadway skirts this small peninsula, and several platforms along the route provide some outstanding vistas of Lake Superior. The views from the huge cliffs are especially spectacular during high winds, when tremendously powerful waves crash against the sides of the deep-brown rocks. Many families also cross the narrow strip of land that connects this day park to Marquette to enjoy a variety of manmade attractions, including a water slide, a marina, picnic facilities and a small zoo.

A few miles west of Marquette, Negaunee (site of Michigan's first iron ore discovery) and Ishpeming lie in the center of the Marquette Iron Range. The area's shaft mines have all closed, but there are a few open-pit mines still in operation. The Empire Mine, in Palmer, is the most active, and you can view the Tilden Mine, south of Negaunee, from a public overlook. The Michigan Iron Industry Museum in Negaunee is the most recent addition to several interesting museums in the area.

Just west of Negaunee and Ishpeming is 6-mile-long Lake Michigamme, whose golden waters and many small islands are very popular with boaters, fishermen and swimmers. Just north of that area, a total of 59 moose were transplanted from Canada by the Michigan DNR in an attempt to re-establish a herd in the Huron Mountains.

Numerous waterfalls are scattered throughout Marquette County. Many, unfortunately, are located on private property. Those open to the public, however, present a wide variety, with accessibility ranging from easy, short walks to strenuous hikes into some of the most rugged, untouched areas of the Upper Peninsula.

UPPER CARP RIVER FALLS (p. 38)

Marquette County

Upper Falls

The falls is located on private property.

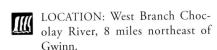 LOCATION: Chocolay River, 2½ miles northwest of Carlshend.

Frohling Falls
(Also known as Chocolay Falls)

This falls is located on private property.

LOCATION: West Branch Chocolay River, 8 miles northeast of Gwinn.

First Falls
Second Falls

The East Branch of the Escanaba River makes two small drops as it flows through a lovely area at a tourist park in Gwinn.

There is a swimming area at the base of the First Falls and a beach along the riverbank. The falls drops only about two feet through a low section of stone that spans the wide river, and its ripples are quickly swallowed up by the stillness of the pond.

A small walking trail, which follows the slow-moving river as it disappears around a bend, leads upstream about a quarter of a mile to another small falls. As you look upstream to a sharp right turn, you can see the small falls cradled in the bend. This falls, too, drops not more than two feet over an isolated section of stone. The river then quickly recovers and becomes as smooth as glass once again. The immense size of the pines that line the opposite bank, their limbs extending over the river, exaggerate the smallness of this falls.

LOCATION: East Branch Escanaba River, Gwinn.

DIRECTIONS: From M-35 in Gwinn turn north at a blinker light onto Iron St. and go about 3 blocks to the Gwinn Tourist Park, in a large fenced-in area on the left. The trail to the falls goes upstream from a beach area on the right.

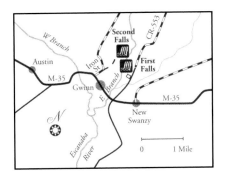

Schweitzer Falls

 LOCATION: Schweitzer Creek, 2 miles south of Palmer.

DIRECTIONS: From From the IGA store in Palmer go south on M-35 0.4 miles to CR-565. Turn right, onto CR-565, and go 1.2 miles to the junction with CR-476. Bear left, continuing on CR-565, and go about 1.5 miles to where the road bears right and crosses a bridge. About 50 feet after crossing the bridge, look for the falls through the trees on the right.

To get to the falls, stay on the high ground on the left (south) side of the river. Use caution in this area; on our visit in 1995 there was no well-worn trail to the falls. And even though this falls is close to the road we recommend marking your route to it with red ribbons.

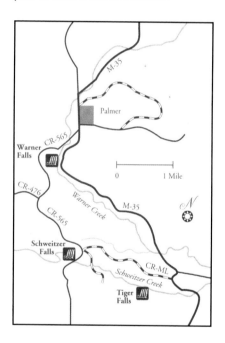

Near Palmer, Schweitzer Creek drops some 30-35 feet in two distinct stages to form Schweitzer Falls. Tucked under the spreading branches of maple and pine that grow from the right bank, the upper falls separates into two streams as it drops about 20 feet. A large flow on the left foams down the black rock, and a small stream on the right feathers out over the shaded stone. At the base of this upper falls they rejoin to form a small pool.

From there, the stream then quickly reaches the lower falls, where it suddenly plunges 10 feet, slides across a table of smooth, black rock, then drops an additional four feet over a scattering of small rocks. A pool at its base casts the reflection of a towering section of smooth, rounded red stone that forms the left bank. A second falls, which can't be seen, creates a disturbance in the surface of this pool on the far side of the rock. The riverbed downstream is littered with small rocks and fallen logs, and as the creek washes over them, the sun reflects off the sparkling surface of the water.

SCHWEITZER FALLS

Tiger Falls

 LOCATION: Schweitzer Creek, 2½ miles southeast of Palmer.

This falls, off County Road ML, is on private property.

Warner Falls

You can view Warner Falls from the side of the highway, but you should also take a short trail to its beginning. There, grassy, flat banks guide the small, clear stream down a few drops and through a channel worn into the iron-colored rock. In a feathery rush of white water the stream drops about 20 feet over the rock shelf, then collects in a shallow pool at the base of the falls before meandering through the underbrush.

The best view of the falls themselves comes from the road about 400 feet downstream from where the trail begins.

LOCATION: Warner Creek, Palmer.

DIRECTIONS: From the IGA store on M-35 in the village of Palmer, go south on M-35 about ½ mile to the falls, on the right.

WARNER FALLS

ELY FALLS

Marquette County

Ely Falls

Though there isn't a formal, well-marked trail to Ely Falls, it isn't too hard to find and is worth the effort.

The route through the woods ends on a huge section of pink-tinged stone with a spectacular view across a valley. Colored cliffs on the opposite side of the large ravine stand out from the greens of the forest, and the crest of the surrounding hills is crowned with a stand of pine, which rises straight from the rock. Below, Ely Creek runs through the center of the ravine but is hidden from view by a thick stand of trees. To get to the river and falls you must scramble down about 35 feet to the base of the rounded wall of rock. A slippery layer of moss partly covers the rock, so watch your footing.

The falls itself is small, dropping a total of about 10 feet in several stages as the creek runs through a thicket of trees and bushes.

LOCATION: Ely Creek, 4 miles southwest of Ishpeming.

DIRECTIONS: From downtown Ishpeming go west on Business Route M-28 past Robbins Flooring Mill, on the left, then another 0.2 miles to Washington St. Turn left (south) onto Washington and go one mile to CR-581. Turn right (west) onto 581 (also called Saginaw St.) and go approximately 2 miles to a fork in the road. Take the left fork (CR-581) and go another 1.4 miles to a blacktop road, on the left just before a brick church. Turn left (east) onto this road and go approximately 2.2 miles to a stop sign at a T intersection.

The ¼-mile route through the woods to the falls begins on the east side of that intersection. We turned right (south) at the stop sign, parked about 200 feet down the road, then crossed the road and found one of several faint trails that lead up, over and down a hill to the falls. As many trails crisscross the area, we recommend that you mark your path on your way to the falls. (We hang red ribbons on trees, then remove them on the way out.)

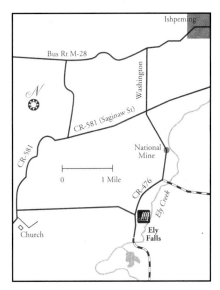

Black River Falls

LOCATION: Black River, 8 miles southwest of Ishpeming.

DIRECTIONS: From downtown Ishpeming go west on Business Route M-28 past Robbins Flooring Mill, on the left, then another 0.2 miles to Washington St. Turn left (south) onto Washington and go one mile to CR-581. Turn right (west) onto 581 (also called Saginaw St.) and go approximately 7.5 miles, across the Escanaba River, to the Black River Pathway on the right. Turn right (west) onto Black River Pathway and go about 0.6 miles to a fork. Take the right fork and go about 0.2 miles to a trail road on the right. Turn right, onto this trail road, and go 0.4 miles to a parking area marked by a line of large stones. The trail to the falls begins on the right hand side of these stones as you face them.

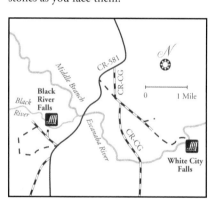

The short, easy trail to Black River Falls winds through such a beautiful stretch of pine forest that the walk would be well worth taking just for itself. However, storms have damaged parts of the walkway, so caution is advised. This area was once a state forest campground, and the remains of long-deserted roads angle off through the stately pines, which stretch far overhead. Though the towering pines command your attention as you walk to the falls, the area is not thickly wooded, and sunlight brightens the entire forest floor. At its beginning the trail is smooth and flat. Then imbedded logs create steps as it drops slightly to cross over the face of a rock bluff and over the edge to the falls.

There, a foaming mass of copper-tinted water cuts between two huge rock bluffs, then tumbles over black rocks hidden in midstream. A small rock outcropping tries to break through in the center of the strong flow, but the water slides over it in waves, covering it with a thin layer of clear water. At the base and in front of this 20-foot-high falls, a large island divides the river into two unequally sized streams. You can cross on a small footbridge to the island for a clear head-on view of the waterfall. As the river widens out on the other downstream side of the island, it forms a small pool whose surface is littered with stray bubbles from the pounding of the falls upstream.

The power of this falls is delicately balanced by its placement in a still and silent landscape. The banks of the river are hedged by dense woods, which thin out dramatically near the huge escarpment of rock that borders the falls. Pale grasses and small ferns peek out from fissures in the side of the rock, whose summit is crowned only with red pine. A light dusting of green moss adds color to the rock and a softness to the falls.

BLACK RIVER FALLS

White City Falls

LOCATION: Middle Branch Escanaba River, 7 miles southwest of Ishpeming.

The falls is on private property.

Caps Creek Falls

The falls is on private property.

LOCATION: Caps Creek, 5 miles south of Republic.

Trout Falls

LOCATION: Trout Falls Creek, 3 miles south of Republic.

DIRECTIONS: We did not visit this falls as there was no trail to it and no room to park on the side of the road near it. However, if you would like to try, here's how to get there: On M-95 from Republic, go south approximately 1.2 miles to a set of railroad tracks. Cross the tracks, then turn right (west) onto CR-601, the first road after the tracks. Go approximately 1.7 miles to Trout Falls Creek. The falls are located about ¼ mile upstream.

Dee Lundeen Falls

The falls is on private property.

LOCATION: West Branch Peshekee River, 5 miles northwest of Champion.

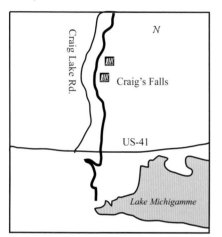

Location: 3 miles northwest of Michigamme

DIRECTIONS: Traveling west on US-41 go 1.5 miles past the Michiggame turn off to Craig Lake Rd. and turn right. Follow Craig Lake Rd. for 1 mile and you will see the falls and pull out on your right. Falls may be viewed from the car. Another small but beautiful falls is a short 500 foot walk back down the road. This falls can also be seen from your car on the east side of the road.

Upper and Lower Craig's Falls

A large rounded section of gray stone seems to grow out of the thin forest of alders and pine, and forces the river to tumble into a small pool before escaping in a frantic run through a fissure, fanning across a large boulder worn smooth by the golden brown water. Beyond this, it's as though the 10 ft. drop hadn't happened -- the river glides gently past gravel banks filled with thick ferns and grasses bending to trail their leaves in the dark water.

Craig's Lower Falls makes a drop of about 5' as the river passes over a shelf of rock in two level sections. The outcropping is so smooth and angular that it could be a stone wall, lying forgotten in the middle of a riverbed. Downstream the river deepens into a dark pool, shaded by the thick forest surrounding it.

LOWER CRAIG'S FALLS

Haypress Falls

Nothing in Michigan is wilder than the Pesheke River as it cuts a swath through towering pine forests and around ancient outcroppings of weathered rock with their sharp corners softened and rounded tops worn smooth. Haypress Falls juts out from a narrow divide in the rock to drive 15' downward, then continues smoothly on before making its final haphazard drop of nearly 30' to the rough water of the river below. Standing at the top of the second drop the course of the river is a study in greens, from the dusty moss stamped generously across the face of the stone outcropping to the deeper, muted hues beckoning from the forest's shadows. This is one of the most beautiful spots in all of Upper Michigan.

HAYPRESS FALLS

 Location: Peshekee River 15 miles north of US-41/M-28, Champion.

DIRECTIONS: About 1 mile west of the entrance to Van Riper State Park, you will cross over the Peshekee River. Turn right (North) on the blacktop road just past the bridge. Go north for exactly 15 miles on this road and park at the turnout on your right. On your left you will notice what looks like a trail starting into the woods but it is just a short turnaround spot. This spot is just before a rock cut that is only on the right side of the road. As you look up the road it will turn to the left immediately after the rock cut. You will be able to hear the falls from this spot. Another aid to checking your location is this: you will pass a road on your right that leads to the McCormick tract 5.7 miles before this rock cut. Also about .4 mile before you reach the rock cut the road splits and a good road goes to your left so be sure that you stay to the right on the Huron Bay Grade. After parking, follow the short trail on your right (east) into the woods. In about 20 feet the trail will split; go left to the top of the falls and right to the bottom of the falls. Both trails are less than 100 feet but if you're going to the top of the falls use caution, especially with children.

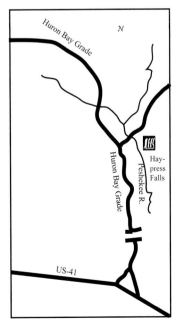

Location: Unnamed creek 5 miles west of Marquette.

DIRECTIONS: Traveling west on US-41/M-28 west of Marquette, turn right (north) onto CR-502 (Midway Drive). Follow CR-502 north for .6 mile to CR-510. Follow CR-510 north for 2 miles to an old iron bridge. Park on the left before crossing bridge. You will find the falls on a small stream emptying into the Dead River about 200 yards upstream from the road. Walk into the woods about 150 feet south of the bridge and walk back towards the river. The trail is next to the Dead River but it is difficult to access right near the river.

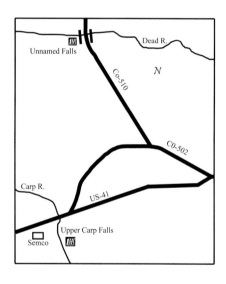

 LOCATION: Carp River, 8½ miles west of Marquette.

DIRECTIONS: Approximately 9.5 miles west of where US-41 and 28 veer left towards Negaunee, you will cross the Carp River. Go past Semco Energy on the left and make a U turn. Park on the side of the road near the Semco Energy building. Follow the fence to the rear of Semco Energy and go left. You will find the trail to the falls there. Go downhill about 200 yards to the falls. Be respectful, however, of the private property in the area.

Unnamed Falls on Creek to Dead River

Near Marquette, the Dead River empties into Lake Superior. Despite its somber name, this river offers many pleasant areas for exploring the natural beauty of the forest. One destination is a little-known waterfall on a small tributary of the Dead River.

From the iron bridge, a 5 minute walk upstream will bring you to the waterfall. It's easier to enter the woods about 100 ft. south of the bridge. Just cross the ditch where you can, and cut diagonally across to the river. The waterfall is about 200 yards upstream.

Although the trail through the woods is fairly easy, the area surrounding the falls is rugged, with sharp outcroppings and tangles of undergrowth at the base of towering pines. With a fallen log spanning the steep banks of the river, the waterfall makes a total drop of about 25' over the rough boulders at the bottom of the crevasse.

Upper Carp River Falls

Although the trail to the falls is overgrown, it can still be easily followed; the sound of the falls will guide you in. The upper falls drops about 8 feet into a roiling mass of white water, then gradually slips away downstream. The view of the river is framed by the fragrant branches of cedars lining the bank. Below, a second falls drops even more dramatically, bordered by the sheer dark walls of a towering cliff dotted with small tufts of grass clinging to its surface. A more welcoming approach is on the opposite bank, where the forest ends abruptly at the river's edge.

Unnamed Falls
Morgan Falls
Lower Carp River Falls

There are four very accessible falls in the Morgan Creek area, all located near the side of the road. Three can easily be reached from one parking area.

The first, Unnamed Falls, is more of a rapids than a falls. As Morgan Creek passes beneath the road (about 400 yards beyond where you have parked), it begins to descend and, in a 100-foot-long section of rapids and small falls, twists and runs swiftly past the thick forest that grows atop the steep banks.

To get to Morgan Falls and Carp River Falls, return to where you have parked. A short walk from the road down a steep bank leads right to the top of the most impressive falls in the area.

Framed by the blackness of wet rock and the emerald greens of the forest, this Morgan Falls is a beautiful sight. It is wide — stretching about 15 feet across the rough stone cliff — and it is loud. The main section drops nearly 20 feet in a brilliant, roaring curtain of white. Dappled sections of sunlight reach between the thick layer of leaves overhead to highlight portions of the rushing water.

The beautiful Morgan Falls area has a few more surprises for the adventurous visitor. Near the falls, Morgan Creek empties into the Carp River, which has more falls and rapids upstream. It's a moderately strenuous hike, but along a pretty ridge forming the bank of the river. The river here has several long stretches of rapids, but about ½ mile upstream is a beautiful waterfall which cascades around two large mossy boulders in midstream, creating ribbons of white as the river drops about 5 ft. Pine branches on the opposite bank dip low towards the water's edge, and upstream you can glimpse the second falls, which also drops about 5 ft.

LOCATION: Carp River, 2½ miles southwest of Marquette.

DIRECTIONS: From the intersection of US-41 and McClellan St., go south on McClellan (which will become Co. 553) for about 2.5 miles to a trail road on the right. This is just before the Marquette Mountain Ski Resort. Turn right (west) onto the trail road and go approximately 1.4 miles to a turnout on the left. Morgan Falls is just down the hill to your left.

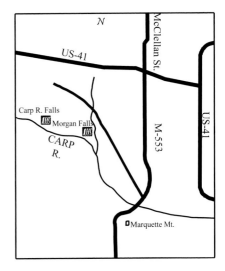

LOCATION: 4 miles southwest of Marquette.

DIRECTIONS: When leaving the Morgan Falls area, continue south on CO 553 for approximately 2 miles to CR 480, turn right. Follow CR480 for 3 miles, and turn right on a blacktop road (CR-NP), which is also marked with a Marquette County landfill sign. Follow this road for about .9 mile and just before reaching the gate to the landfill, turn right on an improved gravel road. Follow this road to the right for about .01 mile and take the trail road on the right. Follow this trail road for approximately .09 mile to a clearing on your left and park in this area. To visit the Upper Falls in this area walk back up the trail for a short distance to the point where an ATV trail crosses over the large pipe on the left. Cross over the pipe and follow the trail to the river, which is about 100 yards. To visit the lower section of the falls, walk back past where you have parked for about 100 yards down the trail and you will see a trail going into the woods on your right. (There is an old stump just off the trail on the right which will help you find the trail.) You will be able to hear the falls from this point. Just head for the river and you will see many trails that lead to the lower falls.

Middle Carp River Falls

The river is so beautiful in this area, and has such a quick drop, that there are falls around each bend in the trail. However, there are three main ones that are particularly beautiful. The upper falls, which is closest to the parking area, is easily 30 feet wide, with a slash of white tumbling out from the forest. Dark boulders divide the flow in the center, and a cache of fallen logs refuse to travel any farther downstream. Below the falls, rapids stretch out in ribbons of white before the river quickly curves out of sight.

After returning to the road, the trail to the next set of falls is about 300 yards down the road and to the right. Children should be closely watched in this area, as the trail rides the ridgeline along the river's course, with steep banks that should be approached with caution.

The next falls is a little more difficult to see, and appears as a splash of white through the greens of the forest surrounding it. Falling about 6 feet, the river again is filled with white water as it courses the rapids on its way to the next impressive drop.

The falls farthest downstream is the most dramatic, with its wall of white rushing out from the shadows of the gorge. Steep banks rise from either side of the river, which drops about 20 feet, twists to the right, and continues to fall for a total of about 60 feet. The river is truly never still in this area; the steep walls of dark rock, capped with evergreens, and a sprinkling of boulders lining the riverbanks creates a beautiful snapshot with every turn in the trail.

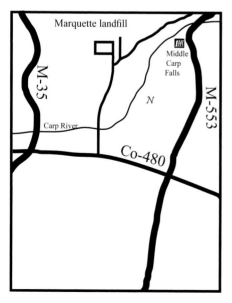

Unnamed Falls

Deep in the shadows of the forest southwest of Marquette, Morgan Creek cuts through a ravine as it meanders to a peaceful, relaxing falls. The water makes several drops — 6 feet at the highest — in lazy streams over and around square sections of rock that resemble an ancient wall. Moss, which covers the flat surfaces of these rocks, provides a soft cushion for the surrounding water as it slips by. Ferns and other delicate plants, which layer the low banks, line the creek with a border of green. This entire area, for perhaps 100 feet, repeats the beautiful pattern of water falling slowly over levels of dark rock.

MORGAN FALLS (pg. 39)

UPPER DEAD RIVER FALLS (pg. 42)

LOCATION: Morgan Creek, 3½ miles southwest of Marquette.

DIRECTIONS: From US-41/M-28 west of Marquette, turn south onto CR-492, just west of the Marquette Mall. (If you are coming from the east, you cannot turn left from US-41/M-28. Go one block farther, make a U turn, return one block and turn right, onto CR-492.) After about 2 blocks the road forks. Continue on CR-492, the right fork, approximately 4 miles to Morgan Meadow Dr.

Turn left (south) onto Morgan Meadow Dr., cross Morgan Creek, then turn left (east) onto the first trail road. Go a short distance on this trail road across a wooden bridge and continue approximately another ½ mile to where the creek again crosses under the road. Just past that point is a small parking area on the right. The trail to the falls begins across the road and follows a ravine that begins where the road crosses the stream.

Note: When you look at a Marquette Co. map, it appears as though you can continue east on this trail road to Morgan Falls, Carp River Falls, and an unnamed falls. We do not recommend attempting a straight-through trip in anything other than a four-wheel-drive vehicle. And even that will not necessarily guarantee that you'll complete the crossing. The trail road is actually an abandoned railroad bed, and two bridges have replaced trestles. It is at those two bridges that the road is at its worst.

We drove a four-wheel-drive truck on our most recent trip to this area, but we still decided to walk. We have walked the entire distance between the two bridges, and there are no waterfalls in that area. Therefore we recommend that you play it safe by following the directions printed in the description of the three aforementioned falls and drive in a short distance on a good trail road.

LOCATION: Dead River, 3 miles northwest of Marquette.

DIRECTIONS: From US-41/M-28 west of Marquette, turn right (north) onto Wright St. (the first street west of Range Bank) and gradually bear right (east) about ½ mile to Forestville Rd. Turn left (north) onto Forestville and go about 2.5 miles, remaining on the paved road as it curves sharply left and reaches a power plant at its end.

The trail to Dead River Falls follows electrical wires up a hill and through the forest behind the powerhouse. About 100 yards past the end of the main hill, a section of an aqueduct is exposed, and on it someone has painted "falls" and an arrow to the left. Follow that trail to the river. (See map, pg. 44)

Upper Dead River Falls

The first falls, about 200 yds. upstream, is framed by leaning cedars and fragrant pines; the river narrows into a powerful flume of white as it courses between the dark rocks forming the banks. It falls about 4 ft., creating a dark pool before contracting again to fall about 6 ft. The trail follows a path above the river's edge, and below the river rushes around huge copper-hued boulders, creating several dark pools before coursing through the white water further downstream.

The second group of falls, a short distance upstream, creates a large forested island as it splits into two cataracts. The left section of falls coursing around the far side of the island is about 10 ft. wide, winding through a series of rapids before falling about 5 ft. in a foamy mass. The stream on the right side of the island has actually split into several small rivulets before returning to the main force of the river for a five foot drop. The river continues full force downstream.

At the falls farthest upstream, a rounded bluff of gray cracked stone emerges from the shaded forest and guides the river as it falls about 20 ft. in an impressive show of force. The dark forest on one bank provides an interesting contrast to the opposite bank of smooth bare stone stretching for nearly fifty feet before being overtaken by the forest once again.

 LOCATION: Reany Creek, 3 miles northwest of Marquette.

DIRECTIONS: From US-41/M-28 west of Marquette, turn right (north) onto Wright St. (the first street west of Range Bank) and gradually bear right (east) about ½ mile to Forestville Rd. Turn left (north) onto Forestville and go about 2.5 miles, remaining on the paved road as it curves sharply left and reaches a power plant at its end.

Just as you pass a bridge before entering the power house area, you will see the bottom part of the falls to the right. There is no parking space at the bridge, so park your vehicle in the power house area and walk back about 200 yards on Forestville Rd. to the falls. (See map, pg. 44)

Reany Falls

As Reany Creek completes its journey to the Dead River, it creates a band of white as it rushes over the rocks in an extensive series of drops. The rock that lines the stream is an interesting mix of rich browns and dark grays, and the greens of the forest shade the entire area. You can see portions of this beautiful little falls from your car. But the falls extends upstream perhaps 200 feet, and you really should explore the trails that run up both sides of the stream.

REANY FALLS

Unnamed Falls on Dead River

LOCATION: Dead River, 1 mile west of Marquette

DIRECTIONS: From US-41/M-28 west of Marquette, turn right (north) onto Wright St. (the first street west of Range Bank) and gradually bear right (east) about ½ mile to Forestville Rd. Continue past Forestville Rd. for another .9 mile to an access road on your left. Turn left and immediately park on your left before crossing the bridge. The falls are above and below the bridge.

The falls above the bridge is a wide banner of white stretching across the 30-foot-wide river, offering a brief taste of what you'll find farther downstream. Below, the river courses between banks covered with shrubs and small trees, its borders strewn with dark boulders. Its steepest drop divides the river, which falls to either side of a small island, its top providing a splash of green mid-stream. The total drop of the river in this area is over 30 feet, and its easy access makes it a very pleasant destination.

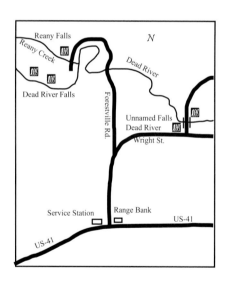

UNNAMED FALLS, DEAD RIVER

Marquette County

Unnamed Falls, Marquette Tourist Park

Anything man can make can be unmade, as happened at the Tourist Park in Marquette. Several years ago, heavy spring rains washed out the dam at the park and uncovered something that had been hidden for decades. Instead of housing a dam with a lake behind, the park now showcases a beautiful waterfall near what remains of the red brick powerhouse. The river widens to about 60 ft. at the top of the falls, and begins its smooth slide to the left over the first ledge of brown stone. Foaming up below that, it straightens out to fall in a foamy white veil before resuming its easy course. The river rushes around several large light brown boulders in midstream before meandering under the two bridges and through the forest beyond.

 LOCATION: Dead River, in the town of Marquette.

DIRECTIONS: From Wright Street on the north edge of Northern Michigan University turn left (north) onto Sugarloaf Ave., which becomes CR-550. Go north for .3 mile and turn left into Marquette Tourist Park. Follow the road a short distance to the baseball diamond and turn right into the parking area. Follow the asphalt trail to the right down to the waterfall. For a handicapped-accessible area, continue past the entrance to the tourist park and to the stop sign, then turn left. Go a very short distance to the bridge over the Carp River. The parking area is on the right just before crossing the river. Park in this area and follow the asphalt trail under the bridge back to the falls. This trail is a short walk and much more level.

UNNAMED FALLS, MARQUETTE TOURIST PARK

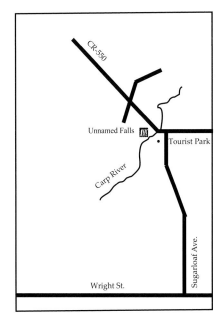

Yellow Dog River Area Falls

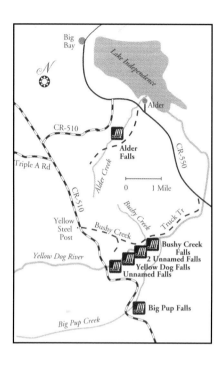

Yellow Dog Falls (also known as Yellow Dog Slate Falls) is the first of several area falls most visitors head to. The trail to it rises steeply through the Huron Mountains to a huge outcropping of rock on the banks of the Yellow Dog River. Directly in front of this outcropping, the falls gradually drops about 20 feet through a deep, 10-foot-wide chasm cut by the river through the stone, then continues downstream in a large section of rapids. The centuries-long pounding of the falls has formed a wide, deep pool at its base, and the surrounding stone shines a wet, glossy black. The banks gradually pull back from the falls and rise to become part of the huge rock outcropping upon which you stand. The bright, almost-white moss that covers this rock mass provides a complementary foreground to the vista's contrast of colors.

A half mile upstream is another impressive but still-unnamed falls that drops about 15 feet as the river rushes around a huge boulder blocking its path towards Lake Superior.

About a quarter of a mile downstream from Yellow Dog Falls is another unnamed falls that drops about 5 feet near a private residence. Continuing along the rocky banks of this

LOCATION: Yellow Dog River, 7 miles southeast of Big Bay.

DIRECTIONS: There are two routes to the falls on the Yellow Dog River. The first (the one we used) is relatively more complicated, but involves a shorter walk. The second is easier to follow but entails a much harder walk.

Route 1: From Wright St. on the north edge of Northern Michigan University in Marquette, turn north onto Sugar Loaf Ave., which turns into CR-550, and go approximately 22 miles to CR-510 (about 2.5 miles before Big Bay). Turn left (south) onto CR-510 and go about 5 miles (bearing sharply left past Triple A Rd. at about 3 miles) to Bushy Creek Truck Trail, on the left directly across from a yellow steel post.

Turn left (east) onto this good two-track and go about 1.4 miles to another trail road, on the right. Continue straight (the road is very bad ahead, so we recommend parking near the fork and proceeding on foot) a short distance to a washed-out area where the trail bears left. Go another ¼ mile to a large clearing of loose sand. It is a short walk down a steep hill on the right, then slightly upstream, to Yellow Dog Falls. On a quiet day you can hear the falls from the top of the hill. An unnamed falls is about ½ mile upstream.

To get to Bushy Creek Falls, continue east on the Truck Trail about 0.4 miles, past a driveway on the right, to the bottom of a steep hill and Bushy Creek. Cross the creek and follow it downstream about 100 feet to the falls, at the creek mouth at the Yellow Dog River. Another beautiful falls is about 50 yards upstream on the Yellow Dog River, and a third is 200 yards upstream, near a private residence.

Route 2: From Wright St. on the north edge of Northern Michigan University in Marquette, turn north onto Sugar Loaf Ave., which turns into CR-550, and go approximately 22 miles to CR-510 (about 2.5 miles before Big Bay). Turn left (south) onto CR-510 and go approximately 6.3 miles to the Yellow Dog River. Cross the river and park on the left. Follow the trail downstream, on the right (south) bank past all five falls, begininng with the unnamed falls at 0.5 miles and ending at Bushy Creek Falls, at 1.8 miles.

wild river, about 200 yards farther downstream is another small unnamed falls, which separates the river into two frothy bands of white before settling into a deceptively calm pool of green-black ripples.

But this river is never silent for long. Just 50 yards downstream, small Bushy Creek descends in a series of short drops—but totaling nearly 30 feet—to meet the rugged power of the Yellow Dog. When we visited in late summer, piles of brush were left stranded far above the normal level of the river. Not only the Yellow Dog, but also Bushy Creek can be fierce when fed by spring melt-off or heavy rains.

The cool greens of the forest beckon invitingly from the riverbank all along this lovely stretch, and the cool water stretches over the black rocks in supple waves. Despite some strenuous walking, waterfall enthusiasts will enjoy spending an afternoon in this area.

Just 1.8 miles south of the Yellow Dog River runs Big Pup Creek, with its own attractive falls. Dropping nearly 30 feet through a narrow chute that zig zags from the highway downstream about 100 yards, the water tumbles past mossy rock outcroppings and shaded banks. Big Pup Falls is bordered by a path thickly shaded with pines and cushioned by their fallen needles. Big Pup Falls is a picture of serenity and solitude.

BIG PUP FALLS

UNNAMED FALLS, on the Yellow Dog River just upstream from Bushy Creek Falls.

BUSHY CREEK FALLS

UNNAMED FALLS, on the Yellow Dog River just below the CR-510 bridge.

Alder Falls

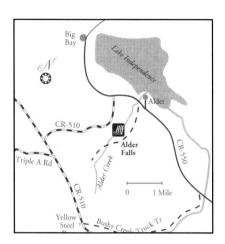

LOCATION: Alder Creek, 2½ miles southeast of Big Bay

DIRECTIONS: From Wright St. on the north edge of Northern Michigan University in Marquette, turn north onto Sugar Loaf Ave., which turns into CR-550. After driving approximately 21 miles (about 3.5 miles before Big Bay) look for a paved road to Alder, on the right. Continue on CR-550 just beyond the road to Alder, then turn left (south) onto a trail road. This trail road immediately forks; take the left fork approximately 0.3 miles to a washed-out area. You may want to park your vehicle in a turnout there, but we continued in a two-wheel-drive truck with no problem.

Whether walking or driving, continue down the trail road for approximately 0.4 miles to the trail to the falls on the right. (If you come to some cottages on the left, you have gone too far.) It's only about .25 miles to the falls, but the trail descends steeply down the side of a hill. The smooth ground is covered with rust-colored pine needles, and the surrounding forest is so thick with pines and hardwoods that only a few smaller trees have managed to poke their way through the branches overhead.

To reach the upper falls, continue past the trail to Alder Falls for .1 mile. The trail to the upper falls will be on your right.

In a series of short drops, Alder Creek falls about 6 feet then plunges 30 feet over the side of a sharply rising rock bluff to create the main section of Alder Falls. The rock bluff seems to come out of nowhere, but looking back through the trees you can see its unusual outline dividing the forest on either side of the falls. The falls covers a 15-foot-wide section of the stony ridge with a blanket of moving whiteness, which contrasts sharply with the dusty greens of the surrounding forest. Above the falls, a few fallen logs have created a natural bridge and a frame, beneath which the water rushes in a frothing mass. At the base of the falls the water bubbles around several large boulders that have fallen to create a necklace of stepping stones.

You can approach the upper falls from the bluff about 40 ft. above the falls. Although you can glimpse the falls, the view is limited. It's also a slippery trail in wet weather, and isn't advised for those hiking with children. Approaching the falls by hiking upstream could be possible, but we haven't tried it, so we can't recommend it.

ALDER FALLS

5 Falls, Big GarlicRiver

The first of several falls on the Big Garlic River is just 50 yards from the roadside. The river drops about 8 ft. amid a scattering of lichen-encrusted boulders. Foliage sweeps back from the shaded banks, creating a thick forest. The smooth trail provides easy access, however, through the dense forest.

A short drive takes you to the second fall in the series. The power of the river begins to show itself here, with clusters of debris trapped several feet above the river. Dropping a total of nearly 20', the river slides over the black rugged boulders, foaming into a small dark pool. A huge fallen log rests at the top of the waterfall, but its smooth ends show the mark of a lumberman's saw, just a remnant from a bygone era.

The third fall dominates a heavily shaded gorge, its steep sides a deterrent from approaching too closely. Making a drop of about 15', the river slides over a smooth patch of rock before plunging through the chute.

The fourth fall begins quietly enough with a small leap and twist to empty into a small pool, deeply shaded by the long arms of maple overreaching the banks. The pool empties through a small opening to slide across a tilted shelf of brown rock, which manages to stay nearly dry, with small tufts of grass clinging to a crack in the stone.

At Big Garlic Falls (just above highway bridge), the river angles again, and courses over a jumble of smaller rocks, passing a level grassy bank and moss-cushioned stones beneath trees leaning close to the waters' edge.

 Location: Big Garlic River, 14 miles north of Marquette.

First waterfall:

From Wright St. on the north edge of Northern Michigan University turn left (North) onto Sugarloaf Ave., which becomes CR-550. Continue north on Co. RD. 550 for about 12.5 miles and you will cross the bridge over the Big Garlic River. Continue for 1.2 miles and turn left on Gold Mine Rd. Follow Gold Mine Rd. for 3.6 miles to a bridge over the Big Garlic river. Cross the bridge and park on the right. You will find the unnamed waterfall across from parking area about 150 feet downstream from bridge

Second, third, and fourth falls:

When leaving the bridge area, head back towards Co.Rd 550 for .8 mile and turn right (South) onto a two track road. Follow the two track for about 100 yards to its end. Walk the trail just to the left about 250 yards to the river. The Upper Falls will be just upstream to the right. You will find the other two distinct falls downstream within 300 yards of the upper falls. Just below the bottom falls you will see a rapids and a cabin across the river. ### Fifth waterfall:

Return to the bridge over the Big Garlic River (on CR550) and park on the right (West) before crossing the bridge. Go up the big hill and follow the river upstream for about .25 mile. There seems to be no defined trail so stay as close to the river as possible to keep from getting disoriented.

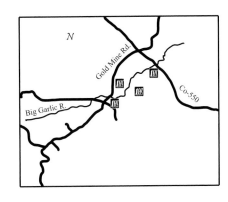

THIRD UNNAMED FALLS, BIG GARLIC RIVER

Little Garlic Falls

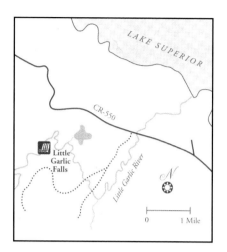

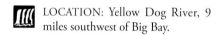 LOCATION: Little Garlic River, 11 miles north of Marquette.

DIRECTIONS: From Wright St. on the north edge of Northern Michigan University in Marquette, turn north onto Sugar Loaf Ave., which turns into CR-550, and go approximately 11.5 miles to the Little Garlic River. Cross this popular trout stream, then turn into a parking area on the left. The falls are about a 2.5-mile walk upstream.

If you have a four-wheel-drive vehicle, you can go on CR-550 another ¼ mile north of the parking area to a trail road on the left. Turn left, follow the trail road about 1½ miles to the river, then walk upstream about a mile to the falls.

Wylie Falls
(Also known as Wylie Falls Dam)

LOCATION: Yellow Dog River, 9 miles southwest of Big Bay.

Access along the main trail to this falls, located about three miles upstream from Pinnacle Falls, ends at a cable strung by owners as a request not to cross their private property.

We searched for about three hours and finally found a way around the private property. However, that route involves a mile hike on an overgrown trail through a remote area. Therefore, we do not recommend visiting Wylie Falls.

Pinnacle Falls
(Also known as Pinnacle Falls Dam)

LOCATION: Yellow Dog River, 8 miles southwest of Big Bay.

By following directions obtained from a local tourist information group, we walked a wide, clear trail to this falls, which is sandwiched between two towering hills in one of the most rugged sections of the Huron Mountains.

We later found out, however, that the falls and trail to it are on private property.

Marquette County

Twin Falls
(Also known as Hogback Falls)

Though this falls is located on a public access road about six miles west of Big Bay, we do not recommend travel to it. The main trail road is generally impassable, and many other trails converge in this remote area.

 LOCATION: East Branch Salmon Trout River, 5½ miles west of Big Bay.

Cliff Falls
(Also known as 40-Foot Falls)

Couched in the seclusion of the Huron Mountains, Cliff Falls is a place of serenity. Tall hardwoods stretch silently overhead to frame the vibrant energy of the river's strong current and the white foaming falls.

The 15-foot-wide river approaches along the face of a steep rock outcropping, then drops at least 40 feet in several stages and in separate streams divided by a section of moss-covered rock. The angle of the falls is steep but not sheer, and toward the bottom it begins to flatten out until it gently meets a pool at its base. A light dusting of bright green moss covers the rough surface of a dry rocky area to the left of the falls. This section is swallowed up by the river in high water, when the falls doubles in size.

 LOCATION: Cliff River, 12 miles west of Big Bay.

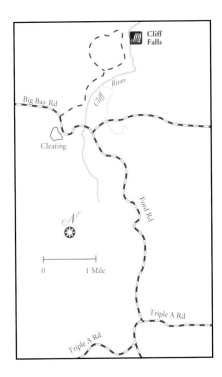

DIRECTIONS: There are two routes to this falls, one from the Big Bay area of Marquette County and the other from Baraga County. We strongly recommend driving to the falls from Baraga County because the route from Big Bay not only takes you through some of the most remote areas of Marquette County, but is also complicated by its intersection with many unmarked trails.

From Baraga County: From US-41 in L'Anse, take Broad St. to Skanee Rd. (Main St.), then go east out of L'Anse on Skanee Rd. approximately 18½ miles to a fork in the road. Take Eric Rd., the right fork, (the left fork is Portice Rd.) past Big Eric's Bridge State Forest Campground (at 1.1 miles), then continue straight ahead across the bridge and follow the main road (Big Bay Rd.) about 6.7 miles to a trail road on the left. (If you pass some junked cars in a clearing on your right, you have gone too far. Turn around and turn right, onto the first trail road you reach.)

Turn onto this trail road (you are on the correct road if, after a very short distance, you see another trail road heading left back to the main road) and go ½ mile past a small building on the right;

CLIFF FALLS

another 0.4 miles past a cabin on the right with a sign reading, "Cliff Falls Hunting Club;" then another 0.3 miles to a beaver pond on the left. Just past the beaver pond, the road forks. Take the right fork approximately 0.9 miles to the top of a hill and a foot trail on the right. Follow that trail down a hill about 75 feet to the river at the top of the falls.

From Marquette County: From Wright St. on the north edge of Northern Michigan University in Marquette, turn north onto Sugar Loaf Ave., which turns into CR-550, and go approximately 22 miles to CR-510 (about 2.5 miles before Big Bay). Turn left (south) onto CR-510 and go approximately 3 miles to Triple A Rd., shortly after CR-510 bears sharply left. Turn right (west) onto Triple A Rd. and follow it about 13.3 miles to Ford Rd., marked by a large clear-cut area just before Triple A Rd. turns sharply left (south). Turn right (north) onto Ford Rd. (a fairly wide, sandy two-track) and go about 4.5 miles (just past a clearing on the left with some junked cars) to the trail road to Cliff Falls, on the right.

Turn onto this trail road (you are on the correct road if, after a very short distance, you see another trail road heading left back to the main road) and go ½ mile past a small building on the right; another 0.4 miles past a cabin on the right with a sign reading, "Cliff Falls Hunting Club;" then another 0.3 miles to a beaver pond on the left. Just past the beaver pond, the road forks. Take the right fork approximately 0.9 miles to the top of a hill and a foot trail on the right. Follow that trail down a hill about 75 feet to the river at the top of the falls.

80-Foot Falls
(Also known as Ives Falls)
River Styx at Ives Lake Outlet

The head frame of the Mather B mine towers over a Negaunee neighborhood in the 1970's. The mine is no longer open, but some of the buildings are being used by the local high school, which is fitting, as their teams are known as the Negaunee Miners.

Middle Falls
Salmon Trout River

Upper Falls
West Branch, Salmon Trout River

Lower Falls
Snake Creek

Mountain Stream Falls
Mountain Stream

These falls — located within the boundaries of the Huron Mountain Club, west of Big Bay — are closed to the public.

Marquette County Dam Sites

Cataract Escanaba Falls

The road to this dam is gated and marked with a "No Trespassing" sign. According to local residents, there are no falls, only a dam, at this site.

 LOCATION: Escanaba River, 3 miles north of Princeton.

Baraga County

An interesting mixture of both natural and historical attractions awaits visitors to Baraga County, which borders the southeastern edge of Keweenaw Bay.

Pointe Abbaye itself, the tip of a finger of land that separates Huron Bay from Keweenaw Bay, is worth a day of peaceful wandering along its trails and Lake Superior beaches. The view from the point is beautiful and includes the elusive Huron Islands, to the east, and the Huron Mountains, to the southeast.

One of Baraga County's mountains, 1,978.82-foot Mt. Arvon, is Michigan's highest point. (For decades, nearby Mt. Curwood claimed the title as the state's highest "peak," but according to official 1985 Geologic Survey measurements, Mt. Arvon is higher by a whopping 11 inches.) At that modest elevation, Mt. Arvon is snow-capped only when winter white blankets the entire county. Snowstorms here can be fierce, but because of the moderating influence of Lake Superior, overall winter temperatures average around 20 degrees,

ERIC'S FALLS (p. 60)

mild compared to the rest of the peninsula.

The land here, however, is rugged and wild, with thick forests spreading south from Lake Superior. An impressive 80% of Baraga County's acreage is open to hunting, and game and wildlife are abundant. If you're lucky, you may even catch a glimpse of a moose. Transplanted Canadian moose were released near Michigamme in 1985 and again in 1987 and since then have spread throughout the Huron Mountain area of Baraga and Marquette counties. One has even been spotted as far east as Luce County.

Baraga County is also home to the Keweenaw Bay Indian Community, and the area is rich in Indian lore and history. For an enlightening experience in Native American culture, attend the KBIC Pow Wow, held at Baraga annually on the fourth weekend in July. Archeological excavations at Sand Point, for example, have unearthed the remains of communities dating from the 12th century. And five miles from L'Anse at the Pinery, the public is welcome to walk through rows of grave sites at an Indian burial ground that dates from the 1840s. Picket fences surround some of the plots, and small wooden houses — their surface weathered by constant exposure to the elements — cover many of the oldest. It's some-how silently reassuring to see the remnants of this burial tradition, which gradually disappeared due to the influence of Christian missionaries.

The influence of missionaries, among the first white visitors to the area, is still felt in other ways. Baraga County, in fact, is named after Bishop Baraga, a Jesuit priest who began the area's first mission at Assinins in 1643. High atop Red Rocks Bluff, between Baraga and L'Anse, stands a unique and beautiful monument to that clergyman and his work. Called the Shrine of the Snowshoe Priest, a 35-foot-high burnished-gold figure of Bishop Baraga — a 7-foot-high cross in his out-stretched hand and 26-foot snowshoes leaning against his side — towers over the wide expanse of Keweenaw Bay. The statue balances on a cloud of stainless steel from which wooden arches swoop down to five teepees, symbols of the five major missions Baraga founded.

Another Jesuit, Father Rene Mennard, came to the area in 1660 and later constructed the North-west's first church at Pequaming, seven miles north of L'Anse. Two and a half centuries later, Henry Ford picked Pequaming as the site for his Upper Peninsula lumber and iron-mining interests as well as his summer home. Today, Pequaming is only a haven for ghost town fanciers.

Big Eric's Falls

(Also known as Lower Huron Falls)

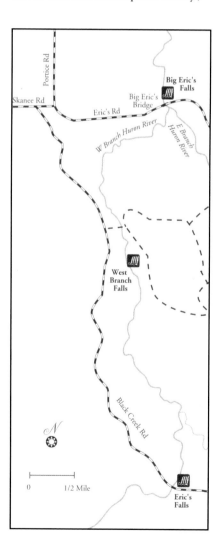

LOCATION: Huron River, 6 miles southeast of Skanee.

DIRECTIONS: From L'Anse go northeast on Skanee Rd. (called Main St. in the city of L'Anse) approximately 18 ½ miles to a fork. The left fork is Portice Rd. and the right fork is Eric's Rd. Take Eric's Rd. approximately 1.2 miles to Big Eric's Bridge Campground. The falls begins at the bridge and runs downstream. (Across Eric's Bridge, the road becomes Big Bay Rd., which leads about 6.7 miles to the trail to Cliff Falls in Marquette County.)

Just below Big Eric's Bridge, the Huron River drops in three sections to form Big Eric's Falls (sometimes known as Lower Huron Falls). At the first, the river divides into five streams across its entire width, then drops abruptly about 4 feet over a small ridge. Several yards farther downstream the river contracts and falls again, this time dropping about 5 feet over the smooth stone.

The rocky banks here fall back from the river several feet to form a large, open area around the water, and as the stone dries, this border turns a golden tan. Rocks scattered throughout the water downstream form a small rapids between the second and third falls.

The third and smallest falls divides into three equal sections as it pounds about 3 feet over a rocky ledge. The churning waters below leave a triangle of white, foamy water that gradually trails away downstream. At the side of this falls stands a lone tall pine, its wide branches shading the bubbling water below. Downstream, the river divides around a small, green island covered with trees and bushes that effectively screen the rest of the river from view.

The river here is a popular spot with both fall salmon fishermen and spring steelheaders. When the steelhead run is in full swing, the banks are lined with eager fishermen trying their luck in one of the many pools in this section of the river. Trails head downstream from the bridge along both banks. On the west side of the river is a state forest campground.

BIG ERIC'S FALLS

WEST BRANCH FALLS (p. 58)

West Branch Falls

LOCATION: West Branch Huron River, 6 ½ miles southeast of Skanee.

DIRECTIONS: From L'Anse go northeast on Skanee Rd. (called Main St. in the city of L'Anse) approximately 18.2 miles to Black Creek Rd. (also known as West Branch Huron River Rd.) on the right. (If you reach the fork at Portice Rd. and Eric's Rd., you have gone about ¼ mile too far.) Turn right (south) onto Black Creek Rd. and go approximately 1.6 miles to a trail on the left. Turn left (east) onto this trail and go approximately 0.2 miles to the west branch of the Huron River.

To visit this falls you must ford a river, so we urge extreme caution. Do not attempt to cross during high-water periods or during threatening weather.

Cross the river and take the road up the hill on the right. Go approximately 0.6 miles and park your vehicle on the edge of the trail in one of the few spots wide enough to turn around. It is just a short walk west to the river, but mark a trail for yourself to guide you back out. At the river you may have to walk a short way up or downstream guided by the sound of the falls.

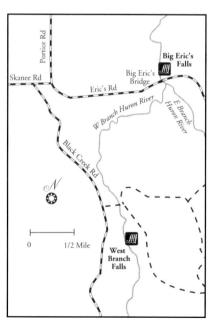

Three distinctly beautiful drops make up West Branch Falls. And as an added adventure, you must ford a river to reach them.

At the first drop, farthest upstream, the 12-foot-wide river narrows to 2 feet as it rushes through a narrow chute it has carved deep into the rock. To the left of this chute, slate banks angle steeply up to a carpet of thick, deep-green moss. Pines, which cling tenaciously to the rocks high up the side of the steep banks, send their thick, dusty-green branches bending over the falls. Downstream, boughs continue to reach over the river from the forest of stately pines and scattered birch.

Just before the second section of falls is one of the best pools we've found for swimming or wading. The river there widens to about 15 feet, and the small rocks and pebbles on the bottom of the pool are distinctly visible through the crystal-clear water. The surrounding banks are not only quite steep, but also — because of countless chipped-out sections — rough. Moss lightly covers some of the stone, causing it to blend into the shadows of the pines above. At the bottom of this long pool the river drops, but only about 2 feet, and the bushy green fronds of thick ferns, which begin to line the banks, brush the cool water.

The river then turns to the left, and heads about 100 yards to the largest falls. There, the river flows over a section of steeply angled stone in a slide of water that drops about 30 feet over the smooth rock. Toward the bottom, the falls splits into three streaks of white against black. A steep bank of rough stone, moss-covered near the top, borders the falls on the left. On the right, huge gray boulders — which seem to have spilled over the side of the falls to line the banks downstream — guides the flow. Also to the right, a small stream that had been separated from the main falls emerges from behind a rock to join with the river once again.

Big Falls

While trying to find this falls, we had to ford the west branch of the Huron River with our truck, which made us even more determined to reach it. The reward was worth the effort.

Surrounded by thick hardwood forest, the east branch of the Huron River flows along the bottom of a gorge it has cut and shaped in its centuries-long rush through the thin layers of stone. In this gorge, the river divides, then drops 20 feet in two sections. The falls on the right forms a near-curtain of white as it drops suddenly from a rough stone ledge. The drop on the left, on the other hand, is gradual. The river there runs over a beautiful section of terraced rock, each step in line with the others to form a perfectly balanced image of layered water. At the base of the falls, the river converges in a large pool, and between the two falls, sections of a brown rock, topped by thick, green bushes, turn light tan as they dry.

Downstream, steep, rough walls of layered stone, which has been chiseled out in bits and pieces by the strength of the river, continue to guide the water.

BIG FALLS

LOCATION: East Branch Huron River, 7 miles southeast of Skanee.

DIRECTIONS: From L'Anse go northeast on Skanee Rd. (called Main St. in the city of L'Anse) approximately 18.2 miles to Black Creek Rd. (also known as West Branch Huron River Rd.) on the right. (If you reach the fork at Portice Rd. and Eric's Rd., you have gone about ¼ mile too far.) Turn right (south) onto Black Creek Rd. and go approximately 1.6 miles to a trail on the left. Turn left (east) onto this trail and go approximately 0.2 miles to the west branch of the Huron River.

To visit this falls you must ford a river, so we urge extreme caution. Do not attempt to cross during high-water periods or during threatening weather.

Cross the river and take the trail road to the left, approximately 2 miles to the east branch of the Huron River. The road turns to the right just as it reaches the river, and the falls are down the steep bank on the left.

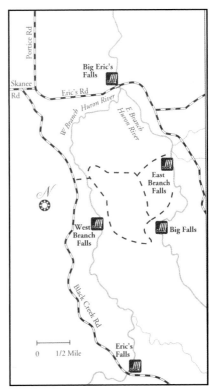

East Branch Falls

LOCATION: East Branch Huron River, 6 ½ miles southeast of Skanee.

DIRECTIONS: Begin by crossing Big Eric's Bridge (directions on pg. 56) The road name changes to Big Bay Rd. Continue 1.7 miles to a small bridge. Cross the bridge and turn right into a parking area. Continuing on foot, walk over the earth berm and down the old logging trail about 1/4 mile. Continue past a large pile of logs to the clearing on the left. At the end of the clearing, there is a trail on the right. Follow this trail about 200 yards to another old logging trail. Turn left on this trail walk another 100 yards to the falls, which will be on your right. The trail is fairly well-defined and easy to follow, but we suggest marking your way in. An alternate way to reach the falls would be to follow the stream from the parking area downstream, and when you reach the Huron River, follow it upstream to the falls. This would be a bit longer, but a more straightforward route to follow.

The Huron River drops about six feet across a rugged outcropping on black stone, creating a foamy carpet of golden hues in a small pond before racing downstream. The banks of the river are covered with saplings, small pines, and larger, mossy trees stretching out over the river. Wherever grasses could find a foothold, they have, lining the river with greens and golds until disappearing downstream and out of sight.

EAST BRANCH FALLS

Eric's Falls

LOCATION: West Branch Huron River, 8 miles southeast of Skanee.

DIRECTIONS: From L'Anse go northeast on Skanee Rd. (called Main St. in the city of L'Anse) approximately 18.2 miles to Black Creek Rd. (also called West Branch Huron River Rd.) on the right. (If you reach the fork of Portice and Eric's roads, you have gone about .25 mile too far.) Turn right (south) onto Black Creek Rd. and go approximately 4.8 miles to the west branch of the Huron River. Cross the bridge and park on your left. The falls are a short distance downstream. (see map, pg. 56)

About 100 feet from Black Creek Road, the shallow west branch of the Huron River drops about six feet over a stone ridge that extends from the water through the surrounding forest. The river divides into delicate streams of white, which course over the smooth, dark stone, then rejoin as they reach for the bottom. The stones that make up the ridge under the falls have developed very interesting shapes. Smoothed out with curving surfaces and rounded sides, they appear to take on some of the liquid properties of the water that courses over them. A fallen log — its base resting near a small pool — spans the falls from top to bottom. Many of the living trees that surround the falls extend precariously over the water's surface. Their branches diffuse the bright sunlight and bathe the falls in quiet shade.

As the river continues downstream, it drops over several layers of flat steps every few feet. The stream remains shallow, and bushy growth pushes out from the forest over the pebbles and small stones that line the low banks.

(Photo, p. 54)

Letherby Falls

The walk to the falls is through a beautiful forest filled with mature pines, cedars, and scattered hardwoods. The sunlight falls in bright pools along the mossy riverbank, and the falls is guarded by towering pines, their roots entwined in the dark stone along the water's edge.

The falls begins with a six foot wide sheet of white cascading beneath a fallen log, then zigzags through the shadows of towering cedars surrounding it. Continuous stairsteps of dark stone, broken at right angles, provide shelves to support the river as it slips over and around its mossy banks. After a total drop of about 50 ft., a shallow pool provides a bit of calm before the river continues its path through the deep forest.

LOCATION: West Branch Huron River, 8 miles southeast of Skanee.

DIRECTIONS: Follow the map and directions on pg. 57 to Eric's Falls. Cross the bridge and turn immediately onto Letherby Falls Rd. Follow Letherby Falls Rd. for approximastely 2.7 miles to a two track on the right. Follow this for about one mile to the road to the falls. When we visited, there was a 4x4 post at this point with Letherby Falls written on it. We followed the road for about 1/2 mile and parked in a clearing on the left. Because of bad road conditions, we walked the two track for about 1/2 mile to the falls.

LETHERBY FALLS

Upper Letherby Falls

LOCATION: West Branch Huron River, 9 miles southeast of Skanee.

DIRECTIONS: From downtown L'Anse, follow Skanee Rd. 16.5 miles turning right on Roland Lake Rd. just before Zion Lutheran Church. Continue for 7.8 miles (the road will turn right at Roland Lake, and change its name to Ravine River Rd.). At 7.8 miles, you will see Hidden Falls off to your right.

Continue another 1 ½ miles; you will pass the sign to Mt. Arvon on the right. Continue to the left on Ravine River Rd. for about 2 more miles where it veers left. There is an Upper Letherby Fall sign here, along with signs for Red Stump Rd. and Big Bay. Go left aout .1 mile; on your left will be an Upper Letherby Falls sign. Just follow the walking trail on your left down to the falls.

There are several falls on the way to Upper Letherby Falls (Ravine River Falls, Hidden Falls, and Unnamed Falls) and you can visit them either before or after your walk to Upper Letherby, but we would suggest saving the bulk of your time for Upper Letherby Falls, which is the largest of the group.

Rushing along a smooth outcropping of black stone, Upper Letherby Falls is a 20 ft. wide swathe of foamy white bursting out of the dark forest surrounding it. Fragrant cedars line the rocky banks, their roots covered with cushions of deep green moss.

Following along downstream, the river takes a 15 ft. plunge over the sheer face of bedrock, carving out delicate circles from an otherwise smooth surface of black stone.

After visiting Upper Letherby, walk downstream about a quarter of a mile to two more beautiful 30 ft. waterfalls. We walked the river downstream nearly a mile, and found several more small falls before the river flattened out.

UPPER LETHERBY FALLS

Baraga County

Ravine River Falls

The river falls over several groups of rock shelves, each spanning the width of the river and flattening out for several feet before falling yet again. The upper section drops about 10 feet, and the lower section about 6 feet, with rapids both above and below. Remnants of huge moss-covered stumps lay along the path, and the far bank consists of a large outcropping of slate, chipping off in smooth flat layers. A tangle of tree roots line the banks above the water, and a tiny springlet jumps out from between the roots to join the large stream below.

RAVINE RIVER FALLS

LOCATION: Ravine River, 3 miles south of Skanee.

DIRECTIONS: From downtown L'Anse, follow Skanee Rd. 16.5 miles turning right on Roland Lake Rd. just before Zion Lutheran Church. Continue on Roland Lake Rd. 2.9 miles to its end at Roland Lake amd go right on Ravine River Rd. for ½ mile to a clearing on the right.Park in this clearing, and go straight west about 400 yards through the woods to the river. There is no defined trail here, so mark your path. On the way to the river, you will cross an ORV trail, which begins beyond where you have parked. The falls are located almost due west from the end of Roland Lake and downstream from where you have parked.

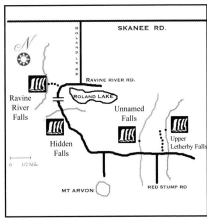

Map to Upper Letherby Falls, opposite page

Hidden Falls

Leaving the Ravine River Falls area and continuing along the road towards Upper Letherby, you can catch a glimpse of Hidden Falls just off the side of the road. Narrow trees line the banks of this small creek, and a short walk will take you to the falls. With just a 5 ft. drop, the stream jumps over its rocky ledge to fan out along the rough stones below. It forms a small pool before continuing beneath the roadway, disappearing into the woods downstream.

LOCATION: Unnamed Creek, 6 miles southeast of Skanee.

DIRECTIONS: From downtown L'Anse, follow Skanee Rd. 16.5 miles turning right on Roland Lake Rd. just before Zion Lutheran Church. Continue for 7.8 miles (the road will turn right at Roland Lake, and change its name to Ravine River Rd.). At 7.8 miles, you will see Hidden Falls off to your right. Pass over a culvert with yellow and black striped signs on both sides of the road. Continue to the top of the hill and park off the road, to your right. The falls are about 100 ft. into the forest on your right.

Unnamed Falls

LOCATION: Unnamed Creek, 9 miles southeast of Skanee.

DIRECTIONS: Pick up the directions for Upper Letherby Falls when it gets to the Big Bay and Red Stump signs. Continue towards Upper Letherby Falls, but stop after about 100 ft. Leave the road, walk about 75 ft. into the woods on the left, and you will be able to hear the falls nearby.

This 10 ft. falls courses its way over the polished black bedrock, creating a smooth surface of water gliding down to the small pool below. The ever-present force of the water has eroded the stone in unique places, creating hollows in its otherwise smooth face. These interesting depressions in the rock add to the overall visual experience.

UNNAMED FALLS

Slate River Falls

White water billows over a ledge of sharply angled rock as the Slate River drops 25 feet. From the base of the falls, a huge, calm pool extends downstream past banks peppered with small light-colored stones. To the left of the main flow, small white strands of water trace their way over this rough stone. On both sides of the falls, the rock has been pushed up to leave a flat surface covered with emerald-green moss. On the left, these rocks rise in several layers, like bright-green steps, to a crest, where pines extend back into the forest.

According to several readers, there are many smaller falls just above the main falls.

LOCATION: Slate River, 3 ½ miles southwest of Skanee.

DIRECTIONS: As you approach L'Anse on US-41 from the south, turn right, onto Broad St., and go approximately 0.6 miles to the blinker light on Main St. in downtown L'Anse. Turn right (east) onto Main and go about 11 miles (Main turns into Skanee Rd. as you leave L'Anse) to the Slate River. Cross the river (just past Arvon Rd.), turn south onto the first trail road on the right, and park. (The Slate River and Slate River Falls Trail are marked with a sign on Skanee Rd.)

The easiest trail to Slate Falls — a half-mile route that follows the west bank of the river — begins across the river from the parking area.

SLATE RIVER FALLS

Black Slate Falls
Quartzite Falls

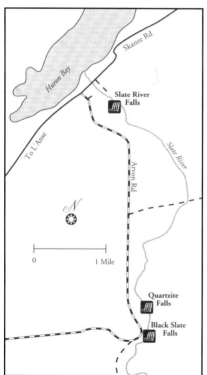

LOCATION: Slate River, 6 miles southwest of Skanee.

DIRECTIONS: Approaching L'Anse on US-41 from the south, turn right, onto Broad St., and go approximately 0.6 miles to the blinker light on Main St. in downtown L'Anse. Turn right (east) onto Main and go about 11 miles (Main turns into Skanee Rd. as you leave L'Anse) to Arvon Rd. Turn right and go approximately 3.3 miles to a trail on the left. (If you reach the point where Arvon Rd. bears sharply right, you have gone just a bit too far. The trail that continues straight from that point leads to the Arvon Slate Quarry area.)

This trail to the river is very short, and though neither falls is marked with a sign, they are fairly easy to find. At the river, look for the remains of an old bridge. Black Slate Falls is a short distance upstream and Quartzite Falls a short distance downstream from that point.

Only a few hundred yards of the Slate River separate Black Slate Falls and Quartzite Falls. The short, easy trail to them runs through forest not thick enough to stop the sun from breaking through the leaves overhead. Slabs of mossy rock are scattered throughout the woods, and occasional wild lilies add a brush of color.

Black Slate Falls begins as a rapids that runs for several yards before dropping four feet over the edge of a rock formation. This main section of falls spans the 20-foot-wide river in three distinct sections, which trail in thin streams over the side of the rock. Mossy rock-lined banks — one softly sloping, the other a sheer wall — guide the water. Downstream, the river forms a chute, through which the water rushes over smooth rock on its few-hundred-feet journey to Quartzite Falls.

The rapids ignores a fallen log in the center as it makes a gradual descent past three strips of grass-covered rock, then rushes to the falls. There, the river curves slightly to the left as it drops over a slate ledge into a pool. The river drops a second, then a third time — about eight feet altogether. Each

QUARTZITE FALLS

Baraga County

section is separated by a small pool, its smooth, dark surface hiding the depths below. Looking back from below the last of the falls, the scene is lovely. A brush of white, the first falls, tops the vista. A band of darkness is then connected through a series of trickling white streams to a second band of darkness. The pattern repeats, until the river finally rushes past and is lost around a bend.

Each falls in this book is surrounded by its own unspoken, unseen history. Quartzite Falls is no different, except that here a bit of history remains in the form of a large hole back from the riverbanks at the top of the first falls. Littered now with rust-colored leaves and pine needles, the excavation blends in with the surrounding forest, and few would notice it. Fewer still would wonder how it got there. The depression, in fact, was a test pit dug by prospectors as a prelude to the Arvon Slate Quarry, which opened in 1872. This quarry had a reputation for providing the best quality slate in the Midwest and was an integral part of the county's economy for many years. Now the hole serves only as a simple reminder of the changing needs of our society.

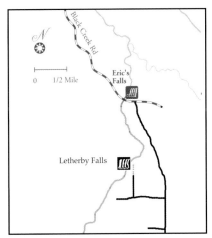

Map to Letherby Falls, pg. 61

QUARTZITE FALLS

Silver Falls
(Also known as Lower Silver Falls)
Unnamed Falls

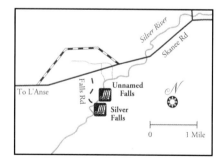 LOCATION: Silver River, 6 miles northeast of L'Anse.

DIRECTIONS: Approaching L'Anse on US-41 from the south, turn right, onto Broad St., and go approximately 0.6 miles to the blinker light on Main St. in downtown L'Anse. Turn right (east) onto Main and go about 6.8 miles (Main St. turns into Skanee Rd. as you leave L'Anse) to Falls Rd. (on the right and marked with DNR Public Access and Silver Falls signs). Turn right (south) onto Falls Rd. and go 0.7 miles to its end. Silver Falls is about 20 feet straight ahead. The unnamed falls is about 100 yards downstream.

Another waterfall (actually more of a rapids than a falls) and a large pool, which is a popular swimming and fishing hole for local residents, is just around the corner from Silver Falls. To get to them, as you leave the Silver Falls parking area turn left onto the first cross trail and go about 100 yards to its end. A trail from the roadway leads a very short distance to the river.

A short trail ends on a huge shelf of rock with a commanding view of the Silver River and Silver Falls. The water below flows through rugged terrain. Huge boulders surround the river, and thick, green forests close in on the flow as it repeatedly drops over even more boulders that litter its path.

A trail down to the base of the falls leads to a more intimate view. As you descend, the rock shelf you left behind gradually rises to top a steep wall of dark stone, which towers over the river, on the right. The left bank, though not as tall, is also steep and rugged, with huge sections of sharp rock pushing the forest back several feet.

The river here pulses through two chutes it has worn into the rock, and a long, thin island of stone remains to separate the two channels. Across the river, to the left, another area of stone, which runs through the pines, probably creates another falls and small island in the spring. At the base of the falls, the river forms a small sandy-bottomed pool — ideal for wading or fishing — then twists out of sight downstream.

As we were about to leave the area, we thought we heard another falls farther downstream. We were right. A hundred yards down the trail, the river froths for several yards down a 3-foot-wide channel, then fans out into a 6-foot-drop of white water over the rough, black rocks below. From there, hedged in by rocky banks and dotted with huge boulders in midstream, the river rushes out of sight.

UNNAMED FALLS, SILVER RIVER

SILVER FALLS

Unnamed Falls

LOCATION: Silver River, 4 ½ miles east of L'Anse.

These falls are on private property.

UPPER POWER DAM FALLS, FALLS RIVER (p.74)

LOWER FALLS, FALLS RIVER

Baraga County

The Falls River is one of the most beautiful stretches of flowing water anywhere in Michigan. It is only about 10 miles long, but in that short distance drops over 1,000 feet in its rush to Lake Superior. The Falls River completes its journey by running through the town of L'Anse, which makes the falls along the stream very accessible and easy to find. If we had to recommend just one river to visit in all of Michigan, this would be it.

Beginning at Lower Falls and ending at Power Dam Falls, we will describe eight separate falls. But the river is rarely calm and still, and because it continuously tumbles and churns over countless drops along its course, the true number of distinct waterfalls can only be estimated.

Lower Falls

The Lower Falls is composed of two falls separated by a short distance.

Closest to Lake Superior, the first is part of a century-old dam. The wide river is compressed through a narrow 5-foot channel in the center of the dam, then drops 10 feet and slides by and over the uneven surface of the slab stone that lines the riverbed below. Most of this rock — its once-sharp crevasses and edges now softened and smoothly contoured — is above water level, and its blue-gray color accents the crystal-clear water as it rushes by. A short distance downstream, the 50-foot-wide river drops another three feet in a band of white, then rushes on in rapids interrupted by occasional dry patches of rocky ledge that span the river.

The beauty of the second Lower Falls, located upstream from the dam about 100 yards, is typical of the entire river. As the stream drops a total of about 12 feet, the water rushes over so many different levels of rock that it appears to be just a constant splash over a blanket of rough stone. On the left looking upstream, the river drops abruptly, as the water falls directly from the top level to the base of the falls. But on the right, the rock bed eases down to the base of the falls, and in delicate white tendrils the river traces the contour of the stone beneath. The colorful blue-gray stone stretches up to line both banks. One large section makes a convenient viewing platform, and on the opposite bank, another slab peers out from beneath the awning of thick, leafy trees and shrubs that line the river on both sides. Birch trees here stretch toward the sky, their whiteness reflected in the dark pool that extends downstream from the base of the falls.

LOCATION: Falls River, L'Anse.

DIRECTIONS: See directions to Middle Falls, p. 72.

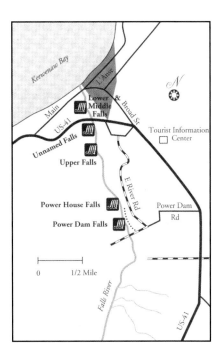

Middle Falls

LOCATION: Falls River, L'Anse.

DIRECTIONS: As you enter L'Anse from the south on US-41, turn right, onto Broad St. (just past a tourist information center on the right). Follow Broad approximately 0.6 miles into downtown L'Anse to the blinker light at Main St. Turn left onto Main and go about 3 blocks, just past a large electrical building on the left, to the Falls River. Do not cross the river, but turn left and park next to it. The trail to the falls begins upstream, just outside the fence around the electrical building.

Certain natural vistas quicken your pulse as you try to take in their beauty. The Middle Falls on the Falls River is one of them.

From the Lower Falls the trail traces its way upstream along a high bluff that overlooks the river. Towering pines stand resolutely on the ridge and frame the river with strength and security. When you first see the falls from this height, it looks like a swatch of fluffy wool, its whiteness contrasting sharply with the black rocks and deep greens of the surrounding forest. Upstream, a railroad bridge spans the river, and from that point, churning white water ducks and bobs downstream about 100 yards to the falls.

Though the river drops a total of 25 feet here, it does so only a few feet at a time. The main section of falls divides, leaving a large section of rough stone in midstream to be covered with the uncompromising greens of thick moss and small ferns. The green is wrapped in a white, watery embrace as the river descends in a double staircase along both sides of the isolated slab.

It doesn't get any better than this.

MIDDLE FALLS

Unnamed Falls

About 200 yards upstream from the US-41 bridge over the Falls River west of L'Anse, a beautiful unnamed falls makes a slow 12-foot descent over flat ledges of black rock. A good view of the falls comes from a railroad bridge downstream.

From there the scene looks like a terraced hillside that has been flooded by a sudden cloudburst. In scattered sections, the 25-foot-wide river drops a foot or two at a time, then flattens out to a shallow, smooth pool before making one more small drop. A banner of thick ferns that covers a dry section of rock in the middle of the falls waves in the breeze, and pine branches sweep down from both banks in an attempt to reach the refreshing water below. A pool that stretches downstream from the falls gives the river a rest from its constant activity.

LOCATION: Falls River, L'Anse

DIRECTIONS: As you cross the Falls River on US-41 on the west side of L'Anse, look south and you will see the falls about 200 yards upstream. Park off the road in the bridge area and walk up the east side of the river to the falls.

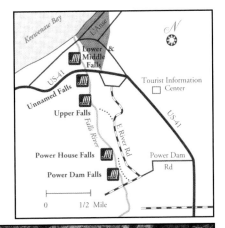

UNNAMED FALLS, FALLS RIVER

Upper Falls

LOCATION: Falls River, L'Anse.

This falls is on private property.

Power Dam Falls

LOCATION: Falls River, 1 ½ miles south of L'Anse.

DIRECTIONS: From US-41 about 1.5 miles south of L'Anse turn west onto Power Dam Rd. and go approximately one mile to the dam site.

The Falls River here was once interrupted by a dam, but all that is left are the forgotten remnants of a sluice way that once carried water to the powerhouse below. A small falls is created as the river courses over a large section of smooth rock on the opposite bank.

Downstream, the river stretches into a large pool, then churns into rapids once again. Also from this point downstream to the mouth of the river is a very popular trout fishing area.

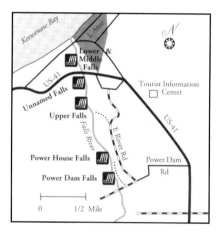

MIDDLE FALLS, FALLS RIVER (page 72)

Power House Falls

For reasons unknown, these beautiful falls have escaped the notice of all but a few people who live in the area.

A five-minute walk down an overgrown two-track leads to a view of a long-abandoned brick power house, which towers over the Falls River. A beautiful border of overhanging maple and pine branches on the opposite bank contrasts with the earth tones of the building, and to the right of the structure, a sparkling 30-foot-wide falls (which we'll refer to as Powerhouse Falls to distinguish it from the second falls upstream) pours over a rock ledge. The river makes several drops behind and around the side of the building before plunging 13 feet in a mass of white foaming water. An opening beneath the powerhouse arches above the surface of the river, and the water there disappears into its blackness. At the base of the falls the river gathers in a wide pool, then continues downstream in an extensive series of rapids.

Upstream, several sections of small drops delicately link Powerhouse Falls with the second forgotten beauty, a large falls that drops about seven feet. The white rush of water there divides around a section of rock, its moist surface dusted with moss and clinging thin grass.

LOCATION: Falls River, 1 mile south of L'Anse.

DIRECTIONS: From US-41 about 1.5 miles south of L'Anse turn west onto Power Dam Rd. and go approximately 0.7 miles (across a railroad track and past East River Rd., on the right) to a trail road on the right. Turn right (north) onto this trail road and park. A gate blocks further vehicle access and you must walk the trail about ¼ mile through a former county park to the old powerhouse and the falls.

POWER HOUSE FALLS

LOCATION: Silver River, 4 miles southeast of L'Anse.

DIRECTIONS: Go south of L'Anse for 0.6 mile and turn left (east) on Dynamite Hill Road. Go 3.6 miles to the fork in the road at the end of the pavement and take the left fork (Arvon Rd.). In 0.3 mile, cross Gomanche Creek. To visit Gomanche Falls, park on the left side of the road as soon as you pass over the creek. Follow the creek about ¼ mile to where it joins the Silver River. After visiting the falls, continue for 0.2 mile to the bridge over the Silver River. Cross the bridge and park, go down the east bank to the falls. It is about 200 yards to the first falls and then an additional 300 yards to the second falls near a house. As you continue along the river by the falls you will come to Page Creek on your right. Here you will see another beautiful little falls as the creek enters the Silver River.

From where you are parked you can also visit a lower falls on the Silver River. About one hundred yards further on Arvon Rd. you will come to a snowmobile trail to the left. Follow this trail into a gravel pit and go to the far left corner of the pit. Go to the top of the hill and you will hear the falls below. The best trail to the falls that we found is just above the falls. The bank is steep in this entire area, which makes it unsafe for small children.

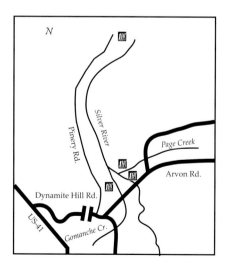

Silver River Falls
Page Creek Falls
Gomanche Falls

From its trip through the open hardwood forest, the Silver River narrows to a quarter of its original width to rush through a small trough. It is framed on one side by a tumble of large black boulders which anchors a grove of saplings, and on the other side with a tilted shelf of stone littered with leaves and small tufts of grass. The river continues in this way before a final tumble into a black pool flecked with foam. It is quickly joined by a smaller tributary.

On Page Creek, a bare outcropping of slate leaves the forest floor behind, save for a thick carpet of rust-colored needles. The river juts across the sharp-edged stone in a frothy 12' drop. This smaller river then joins up with the Silver River just downstream, and it's possible to stand in the fork of both rivers and enjoy each waterfall.

Farther downstream on the Silver River, the terrain remains steep, and it is hard to see the river in its ravine below the trail. You can barely make out its three distinct drops through the heavy pine branches. The river pushes against a wall of stone, and makes an abrupt turn before disappearing again through the trees.

Gomanche Falls is nearby as well, falling in several stages into shallow pools below in a captivating display. The banks of this small creek are lined with ferns and small pines stretching over the water.

GOMANCHE FALLS

Unnamed Falls, Silver River

When the river reaches the ruins of the old railroad bridge, it concentrates its force into a chute about 2 ft. wide before creating a pool. Beyond the pool, it falls again another 30 ft. A haphazard pile of sharply angled rock sends the water coursing over a dozen paths, with the main body of water sliding to the right before rushing over its last large drop. Again, a pool offers a short rest before the river continues its rough course through the woods and out of sight.

Ogemaw Falls

From a tangle of thick bushes, ferns, and pines, the river bursts over the black rocky lip and descends about 5' in a frothy blanket of white. Downstream, the river nourishes the shade-loving plants and delicate grasses scattered along the banks.

OGEMAW FALLS

LOCATION: Silver River, 4 miles southeast of L'Anse.

DIRECTIONS: Go south of L'Anse for 0.6 mile and turn left on Dynamite Hill Rd. Continue 2.8 miles and turn left on Pinery Rd. Go nearly three miles to its end at the falls and an old railroad bridge. The road narrows in the last ½ mile, but there is plenty of room to park and turn around when you reach the old bridge abuttments.

LOCATION: Ogemaw Creek, 7 miles southeast of L'Anse.

DIRECTIONS: Approximately 1.7 miles north of the Sturgeon Falls Rest Area on US-41, turn left onto Baraga Plains Road. Go 1.5 miles and you will see a pond on your left. Ogemaw Creek comes from the pond and goes underneath the road. You will see the creek on your right. Continue just a few yards to a trail leading into the woods on the right. Turn right onto the trail and park. Walk back down the road and over the creek. Follow the trail along the river downstream for about 150 yards to the falls.

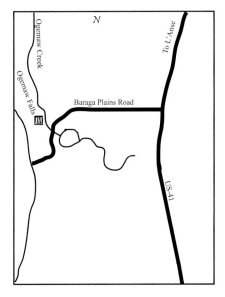

Dault's Falls

 LOCATION: Dault's Creek, 3 miles southeast of L'Anse.

This falls is on private property; we recommend obtaining permission from the owner before visiting.

There is no formal trail to Dault's Falls, so you must "bushwhack it" for about 10 minutes through 300 yards of forest to get to the banks of Dault's Creek and the falls. The effort is worth it.

The creek's 20-foot total fall here begins with a small drop into two small pools bordered by heavy boulders spattered with light-green moss. The water then slides over smooth stone colored with a mixture of browns and cool-gray. Huge sections of shale edge the falls, but the banks downstream flatten into large, soft-green patches of grass. The crystal-clear pools invite wading, and the swiftness of the creek suggests a nice area to try for brook trout.

DAULT'S FALLS

Upper Silver Falls

 LOCATION: 2 miles northeast of Herman.

This falls is not accessible to the public, as the trail to it passes through private property after leaving the main road.

Tioga Falls
(Also known as Tioga Gorge Falls)

We would not recommend attempting to reach this falls because it is on private property that extends on both sides of the river. The signs denoting private property, however, don't appear until you are close to the river.

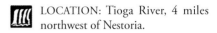 LOCATION: Tioga River, 4 miles northwest of Nestoria.

Unnamed Falls

As the Tioga River runs through a grassy roadside park, the gold-tinged water falls 10 feet in short drops past huge dark-brown boulders strewn in its course. A wood footbridge crosses the river just downstream from the main section of falls. Facilities at the park include picnic tables, grills and restrooms.

Signs near the restrooms point the way to a second, small falls just upstream. From there, follow the trail another 100 yards to another small falls with about a 3-foot drop.

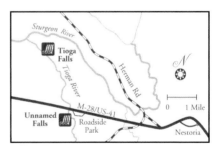 LOCATION: Tioga River, 3 ½ miles west of Nestoria.

DIRECTIONS: On M-28/US-41 go west from Nestoria approximately 3.5 miles to a roadside park on the left (south).

UNNAMED FALLS, TIOGA RIVER

Canyon Falls
(Also known as Bacco Falls)
Unnamed Falls
Lower Falls

 LOCATION: Sturgeon River, 1½ miles south of Alberta.

DIRECTIONS: On US-41 go south from Alberta approximately 1.5 miles to the Canyon Falls Roadside Park, on the right (west). Facilities at the park include toilets, water and picnic tables.

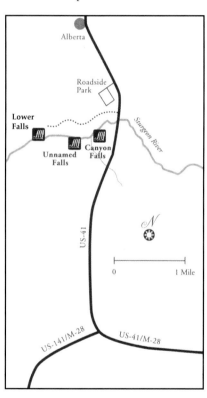

The trail to these three falls penetrates some of the thickest sections of forest in the county. The only visible touch by man along the route is a rail fence that runs along one bank of the river. But if you look over this slight intrusion to the opposite bank, there is nothing else to suggest that this is not what the area would have looked like hundreds of years ago.

The trail to the falls begins at the Canyon Falls Roadside Park. After a quarter of a mile, the path reaches the Sturgeon River, then turns to follow the banks downstream. The river here forms a series of rapids, plus a few scattered miniature falls, then quickens its pace as it nears a canyon ahead.

Canyon Falls, the first falls, drops straight into the mouth of this canyon. The smooth ledge at the top of the falls breaks away into a zig-zag pattern as the white rush of water spills downward about 15 feet over a few rock layers, then plunges into a small pool. Black shadows, which run down the length of the falls, contrast with the golden hues of the rock above, and pale-green moss clings in patches to the smooth rock surfaces. As the walls of the far bank rise steeply, they leave a few narrow ledges striped with green growth. Across the falls, the power of the water has washed a hollow into the rock.

The wood fence that has bordered the river stops at a wall of stone to the right of the falls, and it appears as though the trail, too, ends there. The trail, however, picks up again at the back side of the boulder. Just beyond this rock, look back for another outstanding view of Canyon Falls, gently framed by the dropping branches of soft pines.

The trail then follows the river's high banks along the length of what many have called the Grand Canyon of the Upper Peninsula. Thick stands of pine and fir top the moss-covered walls of stone along the route, and the air is thick with the smell of balsam.

About halfway between Canyon Falls and Lower Falls is an easy-to-miss small unnamed falls. If you pass it as you continue downstream (as we did) look for it on the return trip. Looking upstream it will appear as a distant 8-foot-drop of white framed entirely by the powerful greens of the surrounding forest.

The river continues its rough course through the bottom of the canyon to Lower Falls. There, the 20-foot-wide river slides nearly 30 feet over a large chute of smooth black rock, then splits just before it falls. The section of stream nearest the trail drops in several long stages, and the flow along the opposite bank is screened from view as it drops out of sight behind a thick stone shelf in the center of the river.

Although the falls are beautiful in their own right, the canyon adds an atmosphere of powerful wildness. Guarded by the thickness of the pine forests and the strength of the canyon walls, these three falls will remain a constant in an ever-changing world.

RIVER ABOVE CANYON FALLS

Tibbets Falls

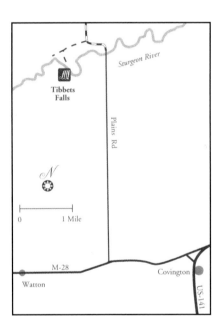

LOCATION: Sturgeon River, 4 ½ miles northwest of Covington.

DIRECTIONS: On US-141/M-28 go approximately 2 miles west of Covington to Plains Rd. Turn right (north) onto the blacktop road and go a little more than 3 miles to the Sturgeon River. Cross the river and continue on Plains Rd. as it bears left a short distance to where it bears sharply right (north). At that point leave Plains Rd. (At one time a sign pointed the way to the falls, but now only a brown post remains.) and continue straight ahead on a trail road approximately 0.2 miles to a fork. Take the left fork and go about ½ mile to the falls. The trail road ends just below the falls, and there is room to easily turn a truck or car around. In wet weather this trail road may not be passable in a car.

Thin fingers of rock extend from the banks of the Sturgeon River to create Tibbets Falls. These unusual projections — which sometimes reach to the center of the 50-foot-wide river — rise above the surface, and each forces the water to make a short drop before running against the next section of rock. Dozens of these narrow strips of rock create drops ranging from a few inches to three or four feet.

CANYON FALLS (pg. 80)

Baraga County Dam Sites

Prickett Falls Dam

LOCATION: Sturgeon River, 10 miles southwest of L'Anse.

There are no waterfalls in this area. You can see the dam from your vehicle but cannot get any closer because all of the surrounding land is posted, "No Trespassing."

Baraga County

Houghton County

Nature has blessed Houghton County, both above and below the ground. This is the heart of the Copper Country. Copper deposits first brought Houghton County to the attention of the world and in turn brought immigrants from around the world to work the area's mines. The frenzied activity here during the mid- to late-1800s rivaled (some say surpassed) that of the more publicized and romanticized California Gold Rush.

Some of the world's purest copper ore was mined here, and at the center of the boom was the town of Calumet, then called Red Jacket. The area, which in the late 1800s supported a population of nearly 50,000, was so prosperous that it literally had more money than it knew what to do with. So the community decided to construct (among other things, such as a 16,000-volume library and the state's first concrete streets) an opera house that would match nearly any other in the country. In 1900 the 1,100-seat Calumet Theater — complete with ultra-modern electric lighting, steam heat and indoor lavatories — opened as America's first such municipally owned facility. Over the next several years some of the period's most famous performers, including Sarah Bernhardt and Lillian Russell, took the stage there. The theater declined with the area's copper industry but in 1974 was restored to its original beauty and reopened to the public. Visitors today can take a self-guided tour or attend a wide variety of scheduled plays and concerts.

Calumet's population now numbers only about 1,000, but the memory of the copper boom is kept alive in an intriguing mixture of tours, relics and museums scattered throughout the county. Calumet's Coppertown, U.S.A. museum and visitor center, for example, is an excellent place to get a thorough introduction to both the history of copper mining in the area and the people whose lives were affected by the changing currents of that industry. Only about five miles south on M-26 at Lake Linden is the Houghton County Historical Museum. That three-story building, once the main office of the Calumet and Hecla Mining Company, is packed with historical artifacts from the entire Keweenaw Peninsula.

Perhaps the most vivid symbol of the power and importance of copper mining in the Keweenaw Peninsula is the Quincy Mine Hoist, the largest piece of machinery of its kind ever used anywhere in the world. In a building next to Quincy Shaft House No. 2, which towers over Hancock on a hill on the north, visitors can examine the giant equipment, which once lifted 10-ton loads of copper ore at speeds of over 36 miles per hour.

A few copper mines — such as the Quincy Mine — remain open to the public for tours. The thrilling experience of walking beneath the earth in an actual copper mine cannot be duplicated anywhere else. The past truly does come to life, and the ghostly echoes of long-ago miners linger in your mind as you reach to touch the cold stone surrounding you. In rock piles around many of the area's long-abandoned mines, it's still possible to find pieces of copper ore.

Many areas throughout the county, in fact, are potential treasure troves for rock hounds. Agate hunters equipped with a good eye and persistence can add many specimens to their collections from the county's Lake Superior shoreline. Isle Royale National Park is also good for rock hunting. Though officially part of Keweenaw County, the island's mainland headquarters is at Houghton, from which boats to the park leave daily throughout the summer season. Another can't-miss spot for anyone even mildly interested in minerals, gems and rocks is the 30,000-specimen A.W. Seamen Mineralogical Museum, which is housed at the Michigan Technological University at Houghton.

That school, which opened in 1886 as the Michigan College of Mines, is one of two seats of higher learning that are legacies of the copper mining industry. The other is Finlandia University. Founded at Hancock in 1896 by the large population of Finnish immigrants who had come to the U.P. to work the copper mines, the school (previously named Suomi College) is the only Finnish institute of higher learning in the United States.

The two sister cities, Houghton and Hancock, are connected by one of the most unique bridges in the state. The entire double-deck span, which has a four-lane highway on its upper level and a railroad track on its lower level, can be raised to allow ships to navigate through on the Portage Canal below. That waterway, which runs through the peninsula from Lake Superior to Keweenaw Bay, is itself unique in that it was largely man-made (again to service the copper industry) and when completed in effect changed the Keweenaw Peninsula technically into the Keweenaw "Island."

And finally, a description of Houghton County would be incomplete without mention of one of its most famous native sons, George Gipp, an All-American college football player who died of pneumonia during his senior year at Notre Dame. Immortalized by the now-famous saying, "Win one for the Gipper," the Laurium native is remembered in his home town by a street-corner memorial and Gipp Memorial Recreation Park.

The bridge spanning the Keweenaw Waterway can lift the roadway and railroad tracks to accomodate passing ships.

Houghton County

Sturgeon Gorge Falls

As the Sturgeon River courses through the bottom of the deepest valley in Michigan, it creates Sturgeon Gorge Falls. This is a powerful river — as much as 78,000 gallons of water per minute rush over the falls — and its scenic beauty is unparalleled.

To see the falls, you must hike to the bottom of the valley. That three-quarter-mile walk is one of the hardest and also most beautiful we have taken to a Michigan waterfall. As the trail approaches the river, it is still far up the hillside with commanding views over the wide expanse of river and wilderness. From there the trees below look like a cushion that will absorb anything that might intrude. The scattered tops of a few towering pines stretch above the rest of the forest to form dark-green conical silhouettes against the blue sky.

The trail then drops to the banks above an upper falls, a

STURGEON GORGE FALLS

LOCATION: Sturgeon River, 10 miles northeast of Sidnaw.

DIRECTIONS: From M-28 approximately one mile west of the Baraga/Houghton County line, turn north onto USFS-2200 (marked by a sign pointing to the Sturgeon River Campground). Go approximately 2 miles on USFS-2200 to a fork. Go right, continuing on USFS-2200 (and following the signs to Sturgeon River Campground) for about 3.6 miles to the Sturgeon River. (As you cross the river, you will see the Sturgeon River Campground on the left.) Continue on USFS-2200 for approximately 7 more miles to USFS-2270, just past where USFS-2200 bears sharply right. (A sign here points left to the falls.) Turn left (northwest) onto USFS-2270 and go 0.6 miles to the trailhead parking area, on the right. The trail to the falls starts across USFS-2270 from the parking area.

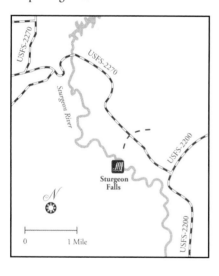

3-foot-high band of white water that stretches 150 feet from bank to bank. To the left of this falls are several small drops, but most of the river falls over the wide, small step. The river here doesn't seem too overpowering, but a glance downstream at huge piles of brush and debris left stranded high on the banks is a vivid reminder of roaring spring currents. Below the falls the river creates a rapids as it passes over countless stones and boulders in midstream.

About 100 feet downstream from that rapids, the river begins to contract to flow through a narrow gorge it has cut into the underlying rock. The river is then forced to concentrate its power as it presses into the 6-foot-wide, 15-foot-long chute. At the end of the stone channel the power is suddenly released, as a curtain of water bursts out and over a layer of rock to fall about 30 feet into a roiling mass of foam below.

An outstanding view of this section of the falls comes from a red rock bank nearly 40 feet above the river. On the opposite bank, heavy tree branches effectively cut out the sunlight. As a result, the boulders that line the banks above and below the falls are padded with a thick layer of emerald-green moss. Downstream, small sections of stones litter the river to create splotches of white in the slate-colored water. Sections of red sand banks spill into the river, and the forested hills of the valley beyond rise up toward the sky.

Duppy Falls

The Jumbo River rushes out from the dense evergreen forest and splits into two sections that dive over a 5-foot cliff of dark bedrock. The frothing bands of white are divided by a damp, mossy section of dark stone littered with fallen branches and home to a few delicate ferns. Upstream, there are other beauties to entice. The first drop is about 6 ft.; the second drop, about 5 ft., remains a few feet wide before suddenly spreading itself over the entire rock face in flounces of lace before joining once again in a pool at the base of the falls. The quiet beauty of the area is compelling, and a visit here can be very soothing.

LOCATION: Jumbo River, 3 miles southwest of Kenton.

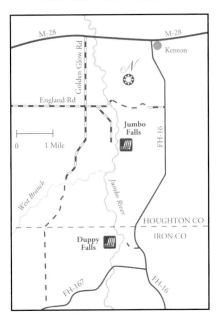

DIRECTIONS: From M-28 on the west edge of Kenton, turn south onto FH-16 and go approximately 4.8 miles to the Houghton-Iron County line. Proceed another 0.4 miles to a two-track road on the right (west). Turn right (west) onto the two-track and follow it 0.3 mile to a clearing. Look for a large slate rock face on the the right side of the trail near the end of the clearing. The trail to the falls starts on the left side of the two-track just across from the slate rock. About 30 yards after starting down the trail, you will cross a small stream. From here the well-used trail meanders through the woods about ¼ mile to the river and the falls, just upstream.

UPPER DUPPY FALLS

Jumbo Falls

The Jumbo River courses softly through the deeply shaded forest floor and, at a perfect viewing spot at the edge of a small clearing, makes a sudden 4-foot drop to create Jumbo Falls. The water creates a frothing mass several feet wide that, when bathed in sunlight, contrasts with the dark shadows of the forest behind.

LOCATION: Jumbo River, 2¼ miles southwest of Kenton.

DIRECTIONS: From M-28 approximately 2 miles west of Kenton turn left (south) onto Golden Glow Rd. and go about 1.5 miles to England Rd. Turn left (east) onto England and go about 0.2 miles east to a fork. Go right (south) on the main road less than a mile to an open area that was once a gravel pit. Continue on through the gravel pit for 0.1 mile. When the two-track re-enters the woods, continue another 0.1 mile to where the road turns sharply right, away from the river (this turn is marked with a sign, because it is part of a snowmobile trail in the winter). Park off the road next to the river and follow the river upstream about 1½ blocks to the falls.

JUMBO FALLS

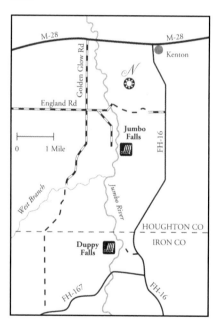

Onion Falls

LOCATION: Onion Creek, 6½ miles northeast of Trout Creek.

Because of the remoteness of Onion Falls and the lack of marked trails to it, we would not recommend a visit.

Sparrow Rapids

As its name indicates, Sparrow Rapids is more of a rapids than a waterfall. An upper rapids drops about a foot as it slides over dark sheets of rock, and the river then descends another five feet in a series of rapids. The swift, shallow flow, with a scattering of small pools, makes the river here a good location for fishing.

These rapids are run by the Sparrow Rapids USFS Campground. Overnight or day-use facilities there include picnic tables, fire rings, toilets and water.

 LOCATION: East Branch Ontonagon River, 3 miles northwest of Kenton.

DIRECTIONS: From M-28 just east of Kenton turn north onto FH-16 and go approximately 0.2 miles to USFS-207. Turn left (west) onto USFS-207 and go 3.2 miles to Sparrow Rapids Campground. Turn left into the campground and park on the right. From the small parking area a sign points the way, to the right, to the trail that leads to steps down a hill about 50 feet to the rapids.

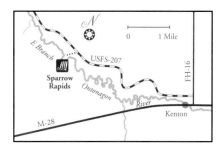

SPARROW RAPIDS

LOCATION: West Branch of the Sturgeon River, 1.3 miles west of Nisula

DIRECTIONS: Traveling north on US-41 in Baraga turn left onto M-38 and go 15 miles to Nisula. Continue west from Nisula on M-38 for 1.3 miles and turn left onto Newberry Rd. Newberry Rd. will dead end in 3 miles at the Sturgeon River where a bridge is out. It is easiest to go to the closed bridge at the river and retrace your drive back up the road for .3 mile to the trail on your right. This is the last trail before you go down the hill to the bridge. The trail is well used and follows the bluff above the river. Follow the trail for .5 mile exactly and park your vehicle. You may be able to hear the falls from this area. Go south into the woods and down the hill to the falls. The walk is about 300 yards to the river.

To visit the last three falls, continue driving down the two track trail for .3 mile to the dirt bank across the road. Park in this area and walk the last .1 mile to a trail road on the right. This trail is an old unused trail to the lowest falls. Walk about 200 yards down this trail and you will be at the lowest falls in this area. There are two more falls upstream each about 150 yards apart.

Hogger Falls, 3 Unnamed Falls

Framed by the thin spires of Maple and poplar, the Sturgeon River descends in a series of delicate steps which span the width of the river. After the quick series of drops totalling about 10', the water settles into a smooth shallow pool before tumbling briefly over a second area of jagged rock. While one bank forms an impenetrable wall of rock, the opposite bank consists of a smooth shelf of rock that rises gently from the base of the falls, but enough to allow a firm carpet of emerald moss to reach out and touch the water's edge.

After a short drive to the lower falls, the first of these falls makes a 12 foot drop which stretches across the entire river. The trail on the high bank provides a good vantage point for viewing the falls, framed by the mossy pines leaning towards the water. Below the falls, the river narrows before twisting out of sight.

100 yards farther upstream, the river makes a sudden twist, falling 7 ft. in a nearly hidden bend in the river.

The final falls upstream is couched in the darkness of a riverbank filled with black stones, where the river divides to fall over a 4' overhang in two distinct sections. The middle, left dry and untouched, juts forward to shade the ground below.

When we last visited this area in 2008, a forest service gate had been erected across the path, making it impossible to drive into this area. It is still open to foot traffic, however.

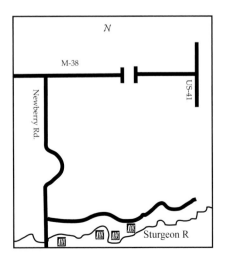

HOGGER FALLS

Vista Falls

We were unable to find Vistal Falls, which are located approximately one mile south of USFS-449 and six miles southwest of Nisula. We made several trips up and down USFS-449 and could not find a trail that led to this falls. We did try three short trails that led south from USFS-449 into a large clear-cut area. However, the trails were bulldozed shut there and did not appear to continue any farther.

Therefore, we do not recommend travel to Vista Falls without current, reliable directions.

 LOCATION: North Branch Sturgeon River, 6 miles southwest of Nisula.

Wyandotte Falls

Only about 250 yards from a parking area the 12-foot-wide Misery River moves slowly out from the forest to fall in several stages over rough, black stone. In the first section, white water drops about 10 feet as it fans down the dark rock, then disappears behind large boulders in the stream bed. After forming a small, hidden pool behind these moss-covered rocks, the stream gradually drops another 10 feet. A soft cushion of moss covers most of the rock surfaces near the water, and pale-green ferns and light grasses creep from the banks toward the water's edge. The forest here is in a damp low-lying area. Moss covers the tree bark, and thick ferns sprout from the earth.

WYANDOTTE FALLS

LOCATION: Misery River, 1½ miles southwest of Twin Lakes.

DIRECTIONS: Wyandotte Falls is located near Twin Lakes State Park, about 20 miles southwest of Houghton on M-26. Coming from the north on M-26 (just past Twin Lakes State Park on the left and a DNR field office on the right) turn right (west) onto Poyhonen Rd. (a sign points to the Wyandotte Hills Golf course). Go approximately 0.8 miles to a parking area on the left. This parking area is just past some old log cabins on the right, which themselves are just past the golf course. The trail to Wyandotte Falls twists through the thick surrounding woods to meet the Misery River about 250 yards from the parking area.

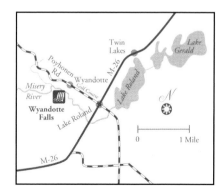

Ripley Falls

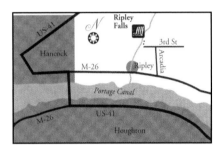

LOCATION: Ripley Creek, Ripley.

DIRECTIONS: From US-41 in Hancock, just after crossing the lift bridge from Houghton, turn right (east) onto M-26 and go less than a mile to Ripley. In Ripley watch for an old brick school building up a hill on the left. Just past that school turn left (north) onto Arcadia St. and go 2 blocks to 3rd St. Turn left (west) onto 3rd and go about a block to where it deadends, just before the creek. Park on the side of the road. The walk to the falls takes only five minutes on a trail that heads upstream to the right.

Ripley Falls is very pretty in the spring or after a heavy rain, but in the summer it is nearly dry. The small stream drops a total of 25 feet as it runs past huge dark-brown rocks that divide the falls into two sections. The area near the falls is deeply shaded by thick woods.

Upper Hungarian Falls
Three Unnamed Falls
Lower Hungarian Falls

LOCATION: Hungarian Creek, 1 mile west of Hubbel.

DIRECTIONS: From M-26 on the southern outskirts of Hubell, turn north onto Sixth St. (marked by a golf course sign) and go 2 blocks to a fork. Take the left fork and travel .4 mile to the yellow gate

Upper Hungarian Falls is tucked into the snug confines of a beautiful hardwood forest, and its frosty white water contrasts sharply with the greens of the surrounding trees. As the falls drops about 25 feet over a sheer wall of reddish stone, separate strands of water trace patterns that reach toward its base. The falls is about 10 feet wide, about the same as the river as it continues to wind its way through the forest.

Downstream from Upper Hungarian Falls, the creek slides over the sheer surface of Hungarian Dam. The stream's natural course here was altered to flow through a channel in the dam. But during periods of high water, the river also follows its original path and in doing so creates an unnamed falls just below the dam on the far side of the river. There in the shade of bushes that line the banks, a small stream of water falls softly over a moss-covered 5-foot red rock wall whose seams and ledges appear so regular and balanced that it looks handmade.

A trail from the dam area crosses over roots and mossy stones as it follows the riverbanks downstream about 100 yards to a second unnamed falls. There, the river makes a graceful descent of about seven feet, then spreads out into a small pool. A low-lying rock shelf stretches out on both sides, and the falls makes a brief splash over the center of the dark stone. You may have to scramble over a few steep rocks to get the best views of this falls.

Downstream another 250 feet, the river again drops, this time in a sheer 25-foot fall broken only by two sections of rock that thrust forward to touch the center of the flow. This unnamed falls creates a beautiful white focal point in a darkly shaded canyon. Scattered bushes dot the face of the high canyon walls, which extend from both sides of the falls, and dark-green moss clings to cracks in the red stone.

About 400 feet downstream is Lower Hungarian Falls, the most spectacular of the five falls in this area. As you walk along the riverbank near the top of the falls, you are close enough to examine in detail the very gradually terraced rock that the river sweeps across. The river drops about 15 feet in this area, and the water creates a pulsing rhythm of life as it courses over the smooth stone.

To view the entire falls, you must walk along the top of the ridge as it extends out from the falls. (Be extremely careful with children in this area.) Through the trees you can catch glimpses of the white-water terraces, then suddenly the entire river shoots out over the side of the ravine in a magnificent 50-foot-plus drop. The thick forest at the bottom of the ravine hides the base of the falls, but traces of its whiteness come tantalizingly into view as it drops through the greens of the trees. And out over the treetops far below, the azure blue of Torch Lake peeks out from the horizon.

There is little along the route from Upper Hungarian Falls to suggest that it will end in such a vista, and the view is all the more breathtaking because it is so totally unexpected.

on your left. Park in this area and follow the trail beyond the gate (about 200 yards) to the mill pond. Continue on the trail about 400 yards upstream to the upper falls. Follow the trail downstream from the mill pond to view the lower falls, which is just below the dam. The three remaining falls are within about ¼ mile from the dam.

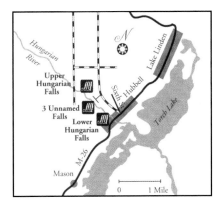

HUNGARIAN MIDDLE FALLS (p. 92)

QUEEN ANNE FALLS

Houghton County

Douglass Houghton Falls

A 10-minute walk along the easy trail to Douglass Hough-ton Falls leads to beautiful sweeping vistas in all directions from the summit of a towering hill. At the crest, a 10-foot-wide stream meanders through grass-cushioned banks, drops a few feet over ledges of square rocks, then disappears over the side of the hill. As you follow along the top of the hill, a can-yon extends outward from the small stream, and it is into it that the water plunges. In a trail of white the creek falls across reddish rocks, clinging to the stone before stretching out from the side of the cliff and plunging nearly 100 feet into the deep canyon below. The canyon walls rise steeply to frame the river with reddish-brown stone.

Barely discernible at the river's edge in the base of the can-yon is an entrance to the long-abandoned Douglas Houghton Mine. The dark hole is filling with stone, and it is only a mat-ter of time before all trace of it will have disappeared.

The smooth hilltop — with the surrounding hills and val-ley stretching out to the horizon, and the dramatic depth of the canyon below — makes an excellent picnic site.

At least it used to. Unfortunately, in recent years the falls has been closed to the public because of the misuse of the land by the many visitors. As with all other private falls in this book, we do not recommend visiting.

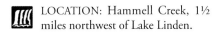 LOCATION: Hammell Creek, 1½ miles northwest of Lake Linden.

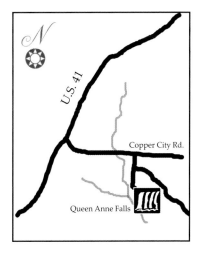

Queen Anne Falls

This is one of the most beautiful falls in the Keweenaw but it takes some effort to get there. The sandy trail descends very steeply to the bottom of the falls, and it's a rigorous climb back up to the top.

Falling nearly 25 ft. down a curving chute between black boulders strewn in its path, the river creates a slash of white to contrast with the dark greens of cedars surrounding its banks. At the base of the falls, a small pool forms before the river races away and around a bend.

LOCATION: Slaughterhouse Creek, 1 mile southwest of Copper City

DIRECTIONS: Traveling north from Allouez on US-41, you will pass a BP station on the left. Just past it, turn right on Allouez Copper City Rd. Go 0.5 mile to the trail on the right. Follow this black cinder trail for 0.4 mile. After passing a small lake on the left, stop and park at the next fork in the trail. Follow the trail straight ahead. The trail turns right along the top of the bluff to the falls. The trail down to the falls is very steep, so caution is advised.

Houghton County Dam Sites

Redridge Falls Dam

LOCATION: Salmon Trout River, 10 miles west of Houghton.

DIRECTIONS: From M-26 just west of Houghton, turn west onto County Rd. P-554/Houghton Canal Rd., which follows the Portage Ship Canal, and go approximately 4.8 miles to the road that goes to Redridge (marked with a sign). Turn left and drive west on that road about 5.8 miles through Redridge to the dam, on the left just as the road crosses the Salmon Trout River.

There is no waterfall at this site, but the dam, which was completed in 1901, is both interesting and very unusual. Instead of cement and other materials common to the time period, pieces of steel, intricately pieced together, were used to construct the dam.

Lower Falls Dam

LOCATION: East Branch Ontonagon River, 5½ miles southwest of Sidnaw.

DIRECTIONS: From M-28 in Sidnaw turn south onto CR-161 (Sidnaw Rd.) and go 2 miles to a gravel road. (A U.S. Forest Service sign there reads, "Lower Dam 4 miles.") Turn right (west) onto the gravel road and go 3 miles to USFS-3500. Turn left (south) onto USFS-3500 and go about one mile to the dam and campgrounds.

There is no visible falls at this location, but the area is very attractive to campers and fishermen. A beautiful USFS campground hugs the shores of the small lake created by the dam. That lake has been stocked with rainbow trout, and the stream below the dam is good for brook trout.

Keweenaw County

Michigan's motto, "If you seek a pleasant peninsula, look about you," is never more apt than when you are standing in Keweenaw County, which comprises the upper two thirds of the beautiful Keweenaw Peninsula. To visitors it seems as if every trail there connects yet another in a long chain of natural attractions.

Brockway Mountain Drive, for example — which twists and turns along the edge of precipitous cliffs from Copper Harbor — is one of the most popular sections of roadway in the entire Upper Peninsula. Built during the Depression, the 9.5-mile stretch of blacktop is the highest above-sea-level roadway between the Alleghenies and the Rockies. People travel hundreds of miles for the pleasure of driving along its curves and hills, especially when the fall color of the thickly forested surrounding hills is at its peak.

If you enjoy wild, unspoiled beauty you won't want to miss Estivant Pines, the last section of privately owned virgin white pine in Michigan. These regal trees, some of which are over 400 years old, were recently saved from the lumberman's saw by the Michigan Nature Association.

SILVER RIVER FALLS (p. 104)

Their 200-acre sanctuary, located near Copper Harbor, is open to the public, and as you meander down the trails, your face shaded from the sun by the tangle of branches extending far overhead, it is hard to imagine that the slender trunks of these few beautiful pines once stretched skyward from just about everywhere in the Upper Peninsula.

Isle Royale is another unspoiled wilderness, this one protected by the federal government, which turned Michigan's northernmost parcel of land into a national park. The 134,000-acre island is a nature lover's paradise, with an untouched beauty all its own and a large wildlife population which includes its two most famous inhabitants, moose and wolves. Moose became a part of the island's fauna in 1912 when Lake Superior completely froze and they were able to cross from the mainland. When the lake again froze solid 37 years later, wolves made the same trek. Isle Royale is also a good destination for rock collectors, who can find Michigan's official gemstone, the greenstone, there. Boats to the island leave daily throughout the summer season from both Houghton and Copper Harbor.

Keweenaw County is not without man-made attractions. On the north shore of beautiful Lake Fanny Hooe, for example, stands Fort Wilkins, the only surviving original wooden army fort east of the Mississippi. Built in 1844, the fort was used sporadically for only a few years before it was finally abandoned in 1870. It is now a state park, and visitors can tour the refurbished and refurnished buildings and other large displays that show what army life was like in the mid-1800s.

Not far away, at the tip of a peninsula that juts out into Lake Superior, is Copper Harbor Lighthouse, its picturesque stone bordered by the blues and greens of the lake. The lighthouse, which houses an interesting maritime-history museum, is accessible only by tour boat.

Keweenaw County also is "copper country," and dozens of long-abandoned copper mines are scattered throughout the area. A few offer guided tours of the dark cavities, whose damp air and empty stillness create an atmosphere so out of place with the former centers of activity and sheer labor. Many of the mines, in fact, gave birth to and nurtured small, secluded communities. When the mines closed, so did the towns. The few buildings left standing in these ghost towns offer only mute testimony to the strength they once had, a strength that was once such an integral part of the Keweenaw Peninsula.

WOODEN BRIDGE IN EAGLE RIVER

Upper Gratiot Falls
Lower Gratiot Falls

The short path to the Upper Falls leads to the crest of a ridge about 40 feet above the Gratiot River, which twists through the trees below. The surrounding forest is very thick, and some trees stretch upward past the cliff edge and trail. Many of the trunks are brushed with flaky, light-green moss that, though it looks like a layer of ashes fragile enough to be blown away in the wind, clings solidly to the bark.

The trail follows the river on the ridge, and its proximity to the edge of the cliff can be dangerous, as the conglomerate stone is continuously being worn away by the elements.

The main drop of the Upper Falls, too, runs over a mass of the conglomerate rock so prevalent in the area. As the river gradually drops about 15 feet, the flow rushes over a myriad of small rocks embedded in the stone to create one large section of shallow white water sparkling in the sunlight. The 20-foot-wide river then forms a large section of rapids as it continues downstream.

Though we did not locate the Lower Falls, we believe that the sure way to reach it would be by walking a difficult route downstream. It is possible, as we did, to get down to the river's edge, but there is no formal trail to the Lower Falls. Fallen trees and thick brush made it difficult to follow the riverbank, and we had to stop after a short distance. We then tried to locate the falls by driving to the opposite side of the river. Again we didn't succeed, this time because of active logging in the area.

LOCATION: Gratiot River, 3 miles northwest of Ahmeek.

DIRECTIONS: From M-26/US-41 just northeast of Ahmeek turn north onto 5 Mile Point Rd. and go about 2.3 miles to Farmer Block Rd. Turn left (west) onto Farmer Block and go straight, a little over a mile, to a trail road. Continue on this trail road about ½ mile to a gate. Park just before the gate and follow the path, to the left, downhill to the Upper Falls.

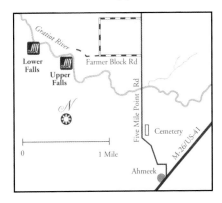

UPPER GRATIOT FALLS

Jacobs Falls

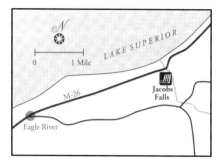

LOCATION: Jacobs Creek, 3 miles northeast of Eagle River.

DIRECTIONS: Go northeast of Eagle River on M-26 approximately 3 miles to Jacobs Falls, on the right.

You can see Jacobs Falls from your car, but it also is a pleasant place to stop, visit and explore. If you look back through the trees from the road, you can see that the falls, though small, has a total drop of about 40 feet. Close to the road, the main section drops about 20 feet in a network of white lines traced over the surface of the rough stone. A border of bare rock keeps the green, bushy woods back from the river. Trails, which run up the sides of the steep rock, lead farther back into the woods upstream. There, mossy banks provide an anchor for cedar trees whose frayed trunks stretch upward toward the light.

JACOBS FALLS

Eagle River Falls

The Eagle River drops over three beautiful waterfalls on its last rush to Lake Superior near the town of Eagle River.

The first, Eagle River Falls, creates a dramatic welcome to the town itself. You can see the falls from your car, but you should stop for a longer look.

The falls is on the original site of the Lake Superior Fuse Co., where the remains of a dam still span most of the 60-foot-wide river. (The plant burned in 1957, and the dam was partially removed in the mid-1990s.) The powerful river slips around the right side of the dam ruins in preparation for a 60-foot drop. Then its forces scatter as the river rushes headlong over the cracked black rock that forms steep banks.

On the far right, a separate, smaller stream, divided by a few hearty trees clinging to the rocks, bounces heavily over the rough stone to join the more-delicate flow of the wider section as it reaches the bottom of the deep gorge.

Upstream are two additional falls, whose quiet solitude contrasts nicely with the larger Eagle River Falls. The closest is Fenners Falls, which is only about 200 feet from the road. However, this is a potentially dangerous area for children, as the easy trail quickly changes to an inhospitable, sometimes hazardous descent over tree roots. At the river, a beautiful rock canyon appears from the depths of the thick pine forest, which threatens to spill over the sheer rock walls of the bank. The upper falls shoots down a narrow path between huge black boulders, dividing into two streams that drop 25 feet before joining again in a dark, narrow pool. The river continues its descent in a second drop just beyond the pool.

Another half mile upstream, a wide, gentle trail leads through the muted shadows of a thick pine forest directly to 10-Foot Falls, so named because it drops 10 feet over the same cracked rock so prevalent in the area. The shadowy banks of the river provide a beautiful backdrop to the mossy rocks and gently falling water. Standing guard at the top of the deceivingly diminutive falls is a majestic pine, its powerful roots providing a secure yet inexplicable hold in the solid rock.

We were informed of the locations of these last two falls by another waterfall enthusiast, Ben Larson, of Trap Rock. Because of his love of the area and persistence in exploring, we are able to share them with you.

LOCATION: Eagle River, near the town of Eagle River.

DIRECTIONS: As M-26 enters the village of Eagle River from the south, it crosses a bridge over the Eagle River. Eagle River Falls is to the right of the bridge, a short distance upstream. For a leisurely view of the falls, cross over the bridge and park on the right.

To visit Fenners Falls, cross back over the bridge and continue south on M-26 about 0.8 mile to two white posts, one on each side of the road, that mark a culvert. Also a two-track driveway is on the right. The trail to the falls begins across from the two-track and leads about 200 feet to the falls. Use extreme care as you descend to the river.

To visit 10 Foot Falls continue south on M-26 about 0.6 miles to a wide turnout on the left. Follow the wide trail a very short distance to the falls.

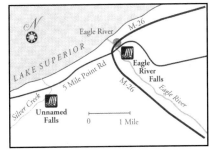

FENNERS FALLS

Unnamed Falls

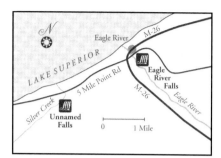

UNNAMED FALLS, SILVER CREEK

This is one of the most beautiful small falls in the Upper Peninsula.

To get to it, take a trail which starts on a ridge then drops down to follow the banks of the river upstream. The small river here runs through a high-walled canyon whose sides gradually slope down toward the water. This conglomerate stone is covered by a carpet of bright green moss whose softness blends with the dark shadows of the forest floor.

Thick branches high overhead allow only a dappling of sunlight to reach through, touching here a branch, there a section of water.

In the distance is a slash of bright, white movement. There the stream drops about 15 feet in a frothy white curtain that splashes over the conglomerate rock. Framed by the deep emerald greens of the surrounding moss and ferns, the tantalizing beauty of this falls has a strong visual impact. The softness of the shaded forest creates an atmosphere of relaxation, and the overall experience is a delight to all the senses.

LOCATION: Silver Creek, 2 miles southwest of Eagle River.

DIRECTIONS: From M-26 just south of the village of Eagle River turn west onto 5 Mile Point Rd. and go approximately 1.7 miles to Silver Creek. Make a U turn before crossing Silver Creek and park on the side of the road. Follow Silver Creek (it runs next to the road for a short distance) upstream approximately ¼ mile to the falls.

10-FOOT FALLS (p. 101)

Copper Falls

Nestled in the deep woods near Eagle Harbor is Copper Falls. An active copper-mining town with the same name once covered an area near the falls, and Copper Creek is said to have passed directly through the mine at one time. The trail to the falls passes a few of the structures that remain in the ghost town.

When we visited in midsummer, the stream was but a bare trickle that fell in a few strands over what appeared to be a 7-foot-high shelf of rock. But when we walked closer, we could see that decades ago, evidently, a log dam had been constructed on the top of the original shelf of rock. The deep-green shadows of thick hanging moss outlines the shapes of the logs in the upper portion of the falls.

Downstream from the dam and falls, the tiny flow of water wanders through smooth moss-covered stones that are dappled with sunlight. Ferns, plus small pines that have just begun to take hold, line the banks.

LOCATION: Owl Creek, 3 miles southwest of Eagle Harbor .

DIRECTIONS: As M-26 enters Eagle Harbor from the west it makes a 90-degree turn to the right (south) at the waterfront. About 2 blocks farther, just past a motel and restaurant, the highway makes another 90-degree turn, this time left (east). At that point turn south from M-26 onto an unmarked blacktop road (which goes to Eagle River) and go approximately 3 miles to Owl Creek.

Cross Owl Creek and go to the second trail road on the left. (This trail enters the main road at an angle from behind and is fairly easy to miss.) Turn left onto the trail road and go about ½ mile to its end. A turnaround there is up a steep hill, so we chose to park at the trail's end and back up a short distance to turn around when we left. The falls are about 30 feet directly in front of the trail road at its end.

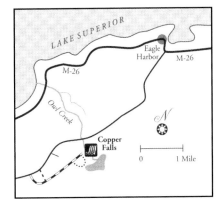

EAGLE RIVER FALLS (p. 101)

Silver River Falls

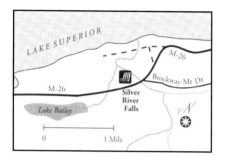

LOCATION: Silver River, 4½ miles east of Eagle Harbor.

DIRECTIONS: From Eagle Harbor go east on M-26 about 4.5 miles to the Silver River (just before the point where Brockway Mountain Dr. intersects with M-26). Park in the parking area on the side of the road and walk downstream to the falls.

Silver River Falls begins just downstream from the M-26 bridge. You can't view the falls from your car, but it is a short, easy walk down the banks of the river. And from a distance the stone arches of the bridge form a perfect backdrop to the falls.

The river is at least 15 feet wide here and, in a series of rapids, rushes over the stone bed toward the falls. On one bank a section of light-brown rock slopes steeply to the water's edge. The opposite side is shrouded in bushes and outstretched tree branches. At the falls, the stream divides to drop about seven feet over a small rock outcropping, then continues as rapids to another sudden drop.

The river splits for a second time, and the rock divider — which remains dry enough to support a layer of wild grasses — is a small island of green in the midst of dark water. After each drop, the river takes a brief respite in a small pool.

Farther downstream, the river narrows to about seven feet and continues on with renewed energy. As we watched it course over a many-terraced section of stone, we were reminded of the fall's name. The water caught the full power of the sun and reflected its light as from one shining block of silver, its sparkling surface sharply contrasting with the deep greens around it. Just past this point, the river cuts a channel into the dark rock and continues through the forest and out of view.

Upper and Lower Montreal Falls, opposite page

SILVER RIVER FALLS

Manganese Falls

The beauty of Manganese Falls is unassuming yet powerful. And it waits patiently for anyone with the time and the inclination to stop by, which is not difficult to do. It is just a few minutes' walk on a trail that runs along the top of a deep gorge. A wooden railing keeps visitors back from the edge, and the tall rock walls completely hide the falls. Then as the trail ends at a viewing area, the sweeping beauty of Manganese Falls comes into sight.

Manganese Creek spills from the top of the gorge, then forms a delicate trail of water as it falls at least 45 feet to the rocky bottom. As the narrow tendrils of water fall, they play hide-and-seek behind the leafy branches that stretch across the narrow canyon. The sheer stone walls are spattered with a pale blue-green moss whose smooth, paper-thin surface forms a soft highlight to the delicacy of the falls. The floor of the small canyon is so thick with trees and bushes that you can only assume that the creek runs through the bottom of the ravine.

LOCATION: Manganese Creek, 1 mile southeast of Copper Harbor.

DIRECTIONS: From the intersection of M-26 and US-41 in Copper Harbor, go east 3 blocks to the Copper Harbor Community and Visitors Center building on the right. Turn right (south) onto the street immediately past that building and go approximately 0.7 miles (past the tip of Lake Fanny Hooe, then slightly beyond where the road makes a sharp right turn) to the falls, on the left. The falls are about 100 feet from the main road.

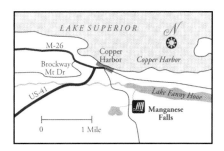

Upper and Lower Montreal Falls

The trail to Monteal Falls follows the beautiful Lake Superior shoreline until you are suddenly at the mouth of the Montreal River, and the Lower Montreal Falls. Three distinct drops surge towards the open water, each forming a small pool before plunging onward. The rugged shoreline is filled with the expected pines and cedars, giving the air a fragrance that is unmistakenly Michigan.

If you follow the river upstream nearly ½ mile, you will pass a small drop before reaching Upper Montreal Falls. Here the river concentrates its force through a 15 ft. chute lined with a cliff on one side and a much smaller angled bank on the other. Small cedars and lichen-encrusted pines cling to the tall cliff, and the dusty blues of the mossy stone contrast with the darkness of wet rock below.

LOCATION: Montreal River, 6 miles east of Bete Grise.

DIRECTIONS: Heading east from Delaware towards Copper Harbor, you will see Lac Labelle Rd. on your right in less than a mile. Turn right and follow Lac Labelle Rd. for 7.2 miles to a trail road on your left. You will soon pass the road to Lac Labelle, which is marked by a large yellow arrow. Continue past this road, and Sand Point Rd. about 1 mile further. 1.9 miles past Sand Point Rd., there is a sign to Smith Fisheries Rd. and Bete Gris Rd. Turn left here, and immediately take the right fork. Follow this improved road for 5.3 miles to Smith's Fisheries. Park at the end of the parking area. From here, follow the road for about ¼ mile. It will become a trail; continue about 2 miles to the lower falls. The upper falls is about ½ mile upstream. *(See map. opposite page)*

Haven Falls

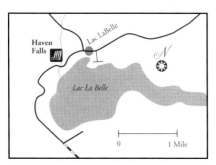

LOCATION: Haven Creek, ½ mile west of Lac La Belle.

DIRECTIONS: From US-41 approximately one mile east of Delaware, turn south onto the road to Lac La Belle. Go approximately 4.5 miles to Lac La Belle, then turn right and go about ½ mile to Haven Park, on the right. The route to the park from US-41 is well-marked with signs.

Haven Falls is small, and its perfection gives it the appearance of being manmade. It's also easy to see. The falls is located at the back of a roadside park but is close enough to the parking area to be seen from a car.

As the small creek runs over the side of a rock outcropping, it stretches white tendrils downward to form a perfectly rectangular block of white against a backdrop of dark stone. Just downstream, a small footbridge, which spans the creek, adds an interesting accent to the falls.

Trails follow the creek upstream, but they are rather steep.

Facilities at Haven Park, which is a beautiful spot for a picnic, include tables, grills and restrooms.

HAVEN FALLS

Tobacco Falls

Starting at the bridge, the river falls over several shelves, the largest drop being about 3 ft. The county park, on the shores of Lake Superior, provide a beautiful little picnic area and a chance to explore both the lake and river. A sandy beach welcomes swimmers, and the bay is framed along its half-moon edge with the whites of birch accenting the dark clouds of pines.

 LOCATION: Tobacco River, in Gay

DIRECTIONS: Traveling north on M-26 in Lake Linden turn right on 9th street. Follow 9th street for about .4 mile and you will cross a bridge over a small stream. Just beyond this point turn left on Traprock Valley Road. Follow Traprock Valley Rd. for about 1.4 miles and turn right onto Gay Rd. Follow Gay Rd. for about 10.4 miles to Gay. Gay Rd. will also be called Laminga Rd. before entering Gay. When entering town follow Gay Rd. left for about .2 mile and turn right onto 2nd Street. Follow 2nd street for about .2 mile to Sherman Twp. Park on your right. The park is just before the bridge over the river and just a short distance beyond the tall smoke stack on your right. The falls can be viewed from under the bridge and continuing upstream.

MIDDLE HUNGARIAN FALLS (pg. 93)

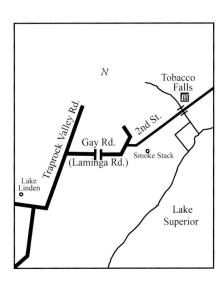

Ontonagon County

Ontonagon County is a paradise for nature lovers, and opportunities for hunting, fishing and other outdoor activities there are almost unlimited. More than 90 percent of the county is forested. Parts of the Ottawa National Forest take up large chunks of the county's acreage, and other sections make up the Copper Country State Forest.

About half of the Upper Peninsula's largest lake, Lake Gogebic, also lies in Ontonagon County, the other half in Gogebic County, to the south.

But probably the county's most well-known natural attraction is Porcupine Mountains State Park, Michigan's largest. Stretching inland from Lake Superior on the county's northwest corner, the "Porkies," as they are called, cover 58,000 acres (including a few in Gogebic County). The "mountains" vary in elevation from 1,000 to 1,400 feet above the level of Lake Superior, and tucked into the folds of these rolling hills are many hidden lakes.

One of the most beautiful is Lake of the Clouds. To most visitors, this elongated section of azure water appears as a slash of vibrant blue that divides the emerald greens of surrounding trees. But for the lucky few who arrive when weather conditions are just right — no wind and a variety of fluffy clouds scuttling by overhead — the lake takes on an amazing beauty. If you peer down into the valley then, you will see, reflected in the glassy visage of the lake, the ivory clouds drifting lazily by in the blue expanse of sky. On these wondrous occasions it truly is a Lake of the Clouds.

More than 85 miles of trails network the park, including many that probe the back country, and backpacking is popular. (Overnight treks must be registered with the park service.) For a truly exclu-sive and remote vacation hideaway, some visitors use the park's limited number of trailside cabins, which can only be reached by a long hike. And the trails in the Porkies, plus hundreds of other miles elsewhere throughout the county, aren't limited to just summer activity. Skiing, snowmobiling, and even snowshoeing are among popular winter sports, which benefit greatly from the proximity of Lake Superior.

Lake Superior makes a powerful statement wherever it brushes up against land, and Ontonagon County is no exception. During the winter the lake is responsible not only for the abundance of powdery whiteness that blankets the area, but also mild temperatures compared to those farther inland. During the summer, visitors can wander Superior's beaches in search of agates or simply rest and gaze across its rough expanse to glorious red sunsets.

Manmade attractions in Ontonagon County include Silver City, the ghost of a brief and unusual part of Michigan's past. In 1872 silver was discovered along the Iron and Little Iron Rivers, and the rush was on. Mines started up along the rivers, and Silver City was founded nearby. But no large pockets of silver were found, and as quickly as the frenzied activity started, it stopped. Four years later the only reminders of the short flurry were tales told 'round a campfire of the undiscovered vein that would rival them all.

The copper-mining boom, too, did not bypass the area. Ontonagon County comprises the westernmost section of the Upper Peninsula's copper range, and it was here that the famous Ontonagon Boulder was hauled from the shores of the Ontonagon River. To area Indians, the estimated ton of nearly pure copper symbolized a manitou, a spirit. To geologists and the copper industry that quickly followed, it represented profit. The Ontonagon Boulder, which eventually found its way to the Smithsonian Institute, was ultimately only a prelude to countless tons of ore that were removed until the rich copper fields were finally and inevitably played out.

The Ontonagon County Historical Museum, in Ontonagon, houses many displays of the area's copper-mining past, and several abandoned mines are scattered throughout the area. One, the Adventure Mine in Greenland, offers guided tours. As we've mentioned in introductions to other counties, a mine tour is an experience you don't want to pass up if you are at all interested in the history of an area.

Another relic of the copper-mining days is the town of Victoria, built near the original site of the Ontonagon Boulder. Like so many Upper Peninsula communities, Victoria lost its spark of life when the copper industry abandoned the area. But unlike other small, almost-forgotten mining towns, Victoria is being brought back to life by a large restoration project aimed at recreating the mid-1800s community as it was at its peak.

Old Victoria, as it is called, is already open to the public, and when you walk across its green lawns past blooming lilacs, the past has never been so near.

ONTONAGON LIGHTHOUSE

Agate Falls

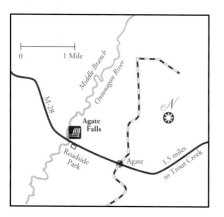

LOCATION: Middle Branch Ontonagon River, 4 miles west of Trout Creek.

DIRECTIONS: On M-28 go approximately 4 miles west of Trout Creek to the Joseph E. Oravec Roadside Park, on the left (south) side of road.

As the sometimes-steep trail to Agate Falls runs over roots and rocks, the middle branch of the Ontonagon River urges visitors on by repeatedly dropping over dark stone to create a chain of miniature falls. The trail leads to a perfect viewing area at the base of the falls. There, the entire scope of the falls stretches out in front of you, and its beauty is captivating.

A cool wind, which usually blows down the length of the river and over the falls, touches the skin with its refreshing purity.

The 80-foot-wide river brushes up against the leafy branches of oaks and maples as it sweeps out of the thick forest to drop over a series of square steps sliced out of stone. Cascades within cascades are created as the water tumbles over the black rock, and a series of soft white trails fall into a pool below. As the river moves slowly over the small stones that fill the shallow pool, it creates a bubbling rapids, then runs through the forest once again.

The trail to Agate Falls begins (and ends) in the Joseph E. Oravec Roadside Park, which is a perfect spot to rest after viewing these popular falls. Facilities at the park include running water, pit toilets and picnic tables.

AGATE FALLS

Bond Falls

Bond Falls, which drops in two sections, is one of the most spectacular in the Upper Peninsula.

In a rush of white water the first drop stretches down the river over flat sections of dark rock. The river widens slightly to about 80 feet and at the center makes an abrupt drop into a small pool, forcing the rest of the falling water to curve around it on both sides. Thick, green grasses brush against the water, and branches from the closest trees bend toward it as it passes. From here, the river curves to the right and disappears behind the trees.

Downstream the banks are lined with a cement abutment to minimize erosion by the strong-flowing river. Water there continues to rush over flat sections of rock, creating a carpet of white all along the area. The cement abutment ends at a viewing platform, which affords an exciting close-up view of the main section of Bond Falls.

The main falls is breathtaking. The water drops nearly 50 feet in a series of step-like drops. The squared-off rock stairs are scattered haphazardly in many different layers, which causes the water to bounce off their flat tops in a complicated pattern of white streams. When viewed from the front, a small grass- and tree-covered island backed by a small section of rock divides the falls into two unequal sections. From the base, the water flows past a scattering of huge rocks, which have fallen from the cliff, to form a large pool that circles out from the falls.

From there the river divides and continues its travels through the shadowed forest. Excellent views of the falls come from two wooden bridges, one spanning each section of the stream.

Facilities near the parking area include picnic tables and a playground for children.

LOCATION: Middle Branch Onto-nagon River, 3½ miles east of Paulding.

DIRECTIONS: From US-45 in Pauld-ing turn east onto Bond Falls Rd. and go about 3.2 miles to a parking area (on both sides of the road) above the falls. There is a handicapped-accessible parking lot just before this, which has ramps leading to the river below the falls.

Cement-block stepping stones span the river, which is just in front of the parking area, and you can view the falls, which begin just downstream from the blocks, from either bank.

At the beginning of the trail a sign warns of the strength of the river and urges caution. Stick to the paths on shore, as the rocks near and in the river are very slippery. Also, swimming and wading are not allowed.

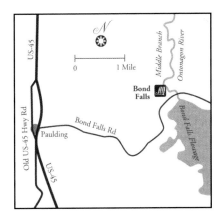

Rock Bluff Falls

We have not been able to locate this waterfall. Initially, after rechecking our topographical maps, we concluded that this falls is marked incorrectly on some maps, which caused us to look in the wrong area. More recent information leads us to believe that this falls does not exist.

LOCATION: Bluff Creek, 1½ miles south of Paulding.

Little Falls

 LOCATION: Middle Branch Onto-nagon River, 4½ miles southwest of Paulding.

DIRECTIONS: Go approximately 3 miles south of Paulding on US-45 to USFS-5250. Turn left (east) onto USFS-5250 and go about 3.7 miles to USFS-4700, on the right, marked by a "4700" written on a brown post. At that point make a U turn and head back west on USFS-5250.

There will be three trails on the right, within 0.2 mile from the point that you made the U turn. Turn right (north) onto the third trail and go about 1.7 miles to the falls, just off the road on the right.

Though there is no formal trail, it is an easy 30-foot walk under towering pines and past patches of feathery ferns and tangles of blackberry bushes to the falls.

There, the 30-foot-wide river drops four feet over sections of black rocks, creating small areas of copper color as the water rushes over the stone. The banks are grassy in most spots, with some underbrush touching the river in others. If you look downstream through the trees you can see the river as it empties into the Bond Falls Basin.

Depending on the water level of the Bond Falls Flowage, this waterfall can be underwater.

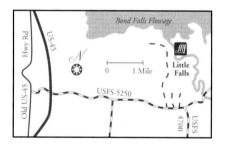

18 Mile Rapids

 LOCATION: South Branch Onto-nagon River, 5½ miles south of Ewen.

The road to this rapids is on private property.

Flannigan Rapids

LOCATION: South Branch Onto-nagon River, 5 miles north of Ewen.

No roads or walking trails lead from main roads to this rapids, and we do not recommend travel into this remote area.

Before you consider taking a trip into any such wilderness areas, we suggest contacting the U.S. Forest Service or the closest DNR office.

Sandstone Rapids

We found no roads or trails that led to this rapids and would not recommend travel to this area.

LOCATION: Skranton Creek, 9 miles north of Ewen.

O-kun-de-kun Falls
(Also known as Baltimore Falls)

As you near this falls, a beautiful foot bridge hangs suspended over the shallow river, joining the lush pine- and cedar-covered banks. Just upstream from the bridge, O-kun-de-kun Falls creates a lacey web of water six feet wide as it glides over the smooth surface of jutting sandstone slabs. The soft, tan-colored stone spreads out from the forest floor, a heavy curtain of towering pines forming a fragrant backdrop. A second falls, which drops about 10 ft. is just upstream. Small bushes have gained a foothold between the layers of rock, adding a dainty touch to the picturesque falls.

LOCATION: Baltimore River, 8 miles north of Bruce Crossing.

DIRECTIONS: On US-45 drive north from Bruce Crossing about 8 miles to a parking area, on the right (east) for the North Country Trail. If you choose to take the North Country Trail, it is well marked with blue markers on the trees, and will take you about 1.3 miles to the bridge over the Baltimore River just below the falls. There are planks over swampy areas of the trail, and the many tree roots make it a bit difficult and slippery in wet weather. Another option is to take the two track that begins at the locked gate in the parking area. This will also take you to the bridge, but is a much easier path.

O-KUN-DE-KUN FALLS

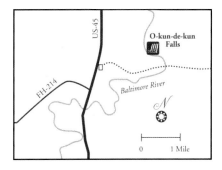

Three Rapids Falls

LOCATION: Middle Branch Ontonagon River, 7 miles northeast of
Bruce Crossing.

Like most rapids in Ontonagon County, Three Rapids
Falls has no access roads or trails and is located on private
property in a wilderness area.

Irish Rapids
Grand Rapids

LOCATION: Ontonagon River, 3
and 5 miles northwest of Rockland.

We attempted to reach both rapids from US-45 northwest
of Rockland. But trails leading to the rapids either had cables
strung across them or were posted as no trespassing areas.

CASCADE FALLS

Cascade Falls

There are two trails to Cascade Falls, the Twin Peaks route and the Valley route. The Twin Peaks trail is longer but more scenic. We took the Valley Trail, which is lower and easier, although it does involve a few steep climbs. Ferns line the path as it laces its way through the heavy woods about a mile to the edge of Cascade Creek. Upstream, huge spire-shaped pines, which border the small river, stretch their green darkness against the sky. And wildflowers, including wild roses that grow along the riverbanks, are scattered throughout the area.

The river here is about 15 feet wide, and as it begins its 20-foot descent, it cuts through a section of bedrock to leave a steep wall for its right bank. As the stream spreads out to the left, it drops five feet, then twists around and over several sections of rock stranded in midstream. Numerous still pools and swirling eddies in this area are good for trout fishing or simply wading on a hot afternoon.

LOCATION: Cascade Creek, 7 miles northeast of Bergland.

DIRECTIONS: On M-28 go east of Bergland 1.2 miles to USFS-222. Turn left (north) onto USFS-222 and go approximately 7 miles (as the road gradually bears northeast) to USFS-831. (Just before this intersection is a "Cascade Falls" sign.) Turn right (east) onto USFS-831 and go 0.3 miles to the parking area and the start of both trails, which are clearly marked by signs along their respective routes.

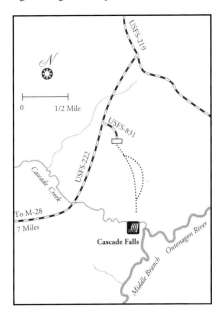

Derby Falls
Hidden Falls

Though the general locations of both falls are included in waterfall lists and a tourist brochure, no one we talked to in the local area knew their specific locations.

LOCATION: Derby Creek, 3½ miles northeast of Bergland and Unnamed Creek, 3½ miles north of Bergland.

Deer Creek Falls
Rapid River Falls

LOCATION: Deer Creek, 7 miles northwest of Bergland and Rapid River, 5 miles northwest of Bergland.

Both falls are in an active logging area on privately owned land criss-crossed by many new roads not shown on maps. We do not recommend travel to these falls.

Little Trap Falls

LOCATION: Anderson Creek, 11 miles south of Silver City.

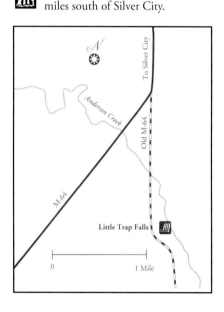

Though there is no formal trail, it's a short walk through the woods to Anderson Creek and the falls. The small river is nestled in the base of a dark, shaded ravine brightened here and there by shafts of sunlight that filter through the overhanging branches. The shallow water drops a total of about six feet over rounded stones cushioned with thick, green moss.

DIRECTIONS: From M-107 approximately ¼ mile east of Silver City turn south onto M-64 and go about 9 miles to the intersection with Old 64. Stay left and go south about 1.5 miles on Old 64 to where it curves left. A short distance farther, the road curves back to the right and, as it straightens out, starts up a hill. Continue up the hill to the first yellow "Caution Pipeline" sign on the right. At that point make a U turn and park on the side of the road.

Head into the woods on the right (east) and go about 300 yards to the third ravine. There is no trail, so don't attempt the walk without a compass and be sure to mark a trail for the trip out. The creek is at the bottom of the third ravine, and the falls are slightly downstream.

Pewabeck Falls

LOCATION: Little Iron River, 1¼ miles southwest of Silver City.

DIRECTIONS: From Silver City go west on M-107 (across the Little Iron River at one mile) about 1.5 miles to a trail road on the left. We were not able to reach this falls because the road was rutted and deep with mud. Before attempting to reach Pewabeck Falls, we suggest that you ask for the latest trail conditions at the grocery store in Silver City. The store owner told us that the road is usually in too bad a condition for anything but a four-wheel-drive vehicle.

Nonesuch Falls

Nonesuch Falls begins with a modest one-foot drop between rough stone banks. The main falls then divides into two separate flows separated by dry rock in the center. Each of the white streams slides 12 feet over the smooth face of the chocolate-colored stone into a pool below. From that 7-foot-deep pool the river slowly meanders out of sight behind a covering of trees.

The thick forest here brushes up against the banks of the 15-foot-wide river, and just above the falls are the remains of the old Nonesuch Mine.

DIRECTIONS: On M-107 go west from Silver City about 2.5 miles to South Boundary Rd. Turn left (south) onto South Boundary Rd. and go about 4.3 miles. Near this point, where South Boundary Rd. bears right, go straight ahead on a narrow gravel road approximately 0.8 miles to the falls.

When we visited, the road was bad, and we were able to drive only about halfway to the falls. The road gave out at a large mud hole surrounded by a large, swampy field, so we parked our truck and continued on foot another 10 minutes to the falls.

LOCATION: Little Iron River, 5 miles southwest of Silver City.

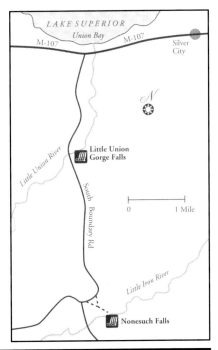

NONESUCH FALLS

Bonanza Falls
(Also known as Greenwood Falls)

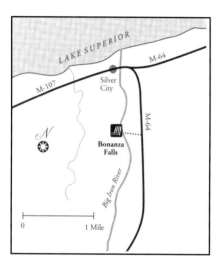

LOCATION: Big Iron River, 1 mile south of Silver City.

DIRECTIONS: From M-107 about ¼ mile east of Silver City turn south onto M-64 and go about one mile to a trail road on the right. Turn right (west) onto the trail and go to a parking area just off the highway. From there, in dry weather you can drive the 0.1 mile to the river; in wet conditions, you may have to walk.

All of our preliminary research had indicated that there was one waterfall in this section of the Big Iron River, so we were surprised and pleased to discover two falls about 200 yards apart.

The rocks that line the riverbed here are some of the most unusual we've seen. They appear to be composed of dozens of layers — which vary in thickness from millimeters to an inch, each colored a subtly different shade of brown — compressed together. As far as the eye can see both upstream and downstream, sections of the banded stone thrust at an angle out of the bed to form a network of walkways across the 130-foot-wide river. From behind, the water cuts away at the diversions as it winds its way through them.

A short distance directly in front of the parking area, the first falls drops about 10 feet through a channel lined with this soft, worn rock. When we visited in July, not much water was flowing over the falls into the deep pool of slow-moving water below. Downstream about 200 yards, the second falls drops much like the first but only a total of about three feet.

These falls would be worth a visit during just about all water conditions. At low levels, more of the unusual jutting rocks are exposed, and during high water the size of the falls increases dramatically.

BONANZA FALLS

Ontonagon County

UNION GORGE FALLS (p. 120)

FALLS ON LITTLE UNION RIVER (p. 120)

ONTONAGON COUNTY WATERFALLS LOCATED WITHIN THE PORCUPINE MOUNTAINS STATE PARK

Numerous named and unnamed waterfalls are located within the boundaries of Porcupine Mountains State Park. The walks to them range from a few feet to lengthy hikes deep into the park's interior. A small portion of the park projects into northern Gogebic County, so descriptions of some of the area's falls are also included in that chapter.

Before you visit the Porcupine Mountains area we suggest that you first stop at the park's visitors center, just south of M-107 on South Boundary Road. There, a variety of helpful maps show the exact locations of waterfalls within the interior of the park, and park employees can provide up-to-the-minute trail conditions.

Union River Falls
Little Union Gorge Falls

LOCATION: Union River, Porcupine Mountains State Park.

DIRECTIONS: From M-107 about 2.5 miles west of Silver City, turn south onto South Boundary Rd. and go 1.8 miles to the Union River. There will be a parking area on your right just after the river. The trail to the falls begins to the north of the parking lot, where there is a sign which reads "Union Mine Trail."

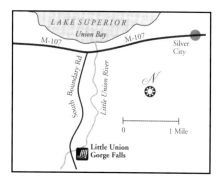

The trail to the falls will make a 1-mile loop, following the Union River until it is joined by the Little Union River. Along the way there are many other beautiful falls too numerous to count. Just upstream from an old iron bridge is Union River Falls.

Although small, Little Union Gorge Falls has a delicate grace all its own. From the bridge that spans the small river, a short walk up the banks brings you to the falls. The upper part of the falls gradually drops about 30 feet over a long section of dark rocks. The river levels out for about 100 feet, then drops another 15 feet as it slides over slightly angled sections of slate. You can walk a bit further downstream and see two more smaller falls. Then go back towards the bridge and continue along the trail.

The trail then turns south to the Little Union River. You will find Little Union Gorge Falls just before the trail crosses South Boundary Rd. The small river tumbles over black rock on its twisted path through the shaded forest, its banks lined with pine boughs reaching out over the rock.

Trap Falls
(Formerly called Epidote Falls)

LOCATION: Carp River, Porcupine Mountains State Park.

Because it is located deep in the interior of the park, anyone attempting to visit this falls should get reliable directions and latest trail conditions at the visitors center.

Ontonagon County

Overlooked Falls
Greenstone Falls

Because of a variety of interesting bridges, walkways and benches built by the DNR, the short trail to Overlooked and Greenstone Falls (and several small falls between them) is one of the most unique and fun that we've walked. Where the easy-to-follow path crosses damp, swampy sections of land, for example, boards have been laid to form walkways. Log bridges — one which has boards nailed across its flattened top, plus a small rope handrail on one side — traverse some areas.

But the most unique feature of this trail, which curves among the towering pines of the Porcupine Mountains, comes when it crosses over the river. The DNR flattened one of the fallen gigantic pines on one side and used it as an 80-foot-long bridge. At both ends small logs form steps up to the unusual span. But there are no handrails. They really aren't needed because the log is so wide. From that crossing you can get a good view of the gorge — its huge banks of earth towering overhead — that the trail winds through.

At about a quarter mile, the trail reaches beautiful Overlooked Falls. There, the 12-foot-wide stream delicately drops past the moss-fringed rocks that line its banks. In a slash of white against the dark stone, the stream drops about four feet to form a small pool, then arches in two sections around a slab of dry rock in the center. Dappled sunlight spills through the thick branches of lofty pines to highlight sections of the mossy rock that edge the river. The pines cling tenaciously to the rock border and here and there send out roots to touch the water.

Less then a mile downstream, the trail approaches Greenstone Falls on a high ridge just upstream from the Greenstone Cabin, available to rent through the Porcupine Mountains State Park. Though the path doesn't drop to the riverbanks, the view of the falls from the top of the gorge is beautiful. The Little Carp River here drops about six feet in several sparkling tendrils. A spectacular covering of thick moss on the small stones that line the banks seems to cushion the impact of the water as it glides gracefully over them. The entire area is thickly shaded by towering pines, which allow sunlight to lightly touch only small sections of the velvet moss.

 LOCATION: Little Carp River, Porcupine Mountains State Park.

DIRECTIONS: From M-107 about 2.5 miles west of Silver City turn south onto South Boundary Rd. and go approximately 18 miles (as the road bears west) to the Little Carp River Rd. Turn right (north) onto Little Carp River Rd. and go 0.5 miles to a parking area. Do not cross the foot bridge that crosses the river at the parking area, but rather, walk downstream on the near side of the river.

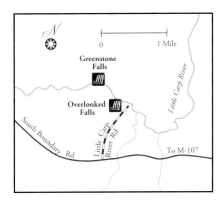

Little Iron Falls

LOCATION: Little Iron River, Porcupine Mountains State Park.

This falls is in the interior section of the park in the White Pine Extension Camp area. Because of its remoteness, anyone attempting to visit this falls should first stop at the visitors center for reliable directions and trail conditions.

END OF ONTONAGON COUNTY WATERFALLS IN THE PORCUPINE MOUNTAINS STATE PARK

Minnewawa Falls
Nimikon Falls

LOCATION: Presque Isle River, 4½ miles northwest of Tula (Gogebic Co.).

According to Jerry Dennis and Craig Date, authors of *Canoeing Michigan Rivers*, Minnewawa Falls is a series of ledge drops and chutes that are forced between car- and house-size boulders to a large pond-size pool at the bottom. Nimikon Falls, according to the pair, is a 12- to 15-foot drop that all but experienced kayakers should portage around.

We have mentioned their observations because we were unable to find either of the falls by land, although we spent the better part of a day searching for them. Our maps seemed to be accurate but did not include many new roads in the area. We also encountered other difficulties. Just west of Tula we turned north from M-28 onto USFS-210 but had to stop after about a mile because a bridge was out. From Jack Spur, about 3¼ miles east of Tula on M-28, we went north on USFS-210 After more than 10 miles of driving through the woods we came to an active logging area, and the road from there was too rough, rutted and rocky to negotiate in our two-wheel-drive truck.

Therefore, even with good, up-to-date maps we would not recommend travel into this area.

Ontonagon County Dam Sites

Victoria Falls Dam

Once a unique and beautiful dam, Victoria Falls Dam has recently been renovated into a very utilitarian shape.

But if you are in the area, visit the restored town site of Old Victoria (See page 109 for details). While in this area you can also search for pieces of copper in the rock piles near the old Victoria Mine site.

DIRECTIONS: From US-45 just south of Rockland, turn west onto Victoria Rd. (marked with a sign pointing to Old Victoria). Go approximately 4 miles on Victoria Road to the town site of Victoria. Near the Ontonagon River, about halfway between Rockland and Victoria, look for some high-tension wires that cross the road. Under them on a small stream that empties into the Ontonagon on the west side of the road is a miniature unnamed waterfall. To get to the dam, continue past the town site about one mile to the end of the road.

 LOCATION: West Branch Ontonagon River, 3 miles south of Rockland.

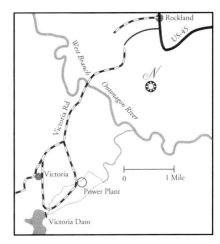

Gogebic County

In the language of the Chippewa Indians, Gogebic means "where trout rising to the surface make rings on still waters." The persuasive call of the beautiful, untainted natural sights that inspired that graceful phrase centuries ago still lures visitors to this lovely area. More than 315 named lakes and over 1,200 miles of streams lie within the county's borders, and there is an abundance of opportunities for fishing, swimming and boating. Winter sports, particularly skiing and snowmobiling, are also drawing cards to the area.

Over 80 percent of the county's acreage is within the boundaries of the Ottawa National Forest, and most of that land is open to the public.

One of the largest parcels is the 21,000-acre Sylvania Recreation Area, near Watersmeet. To help protect the pristine natural beauty of this tract's clear lakes and streams and lush surrounding forest, motorized traffic on land is prohibited in most areas, and boats with motors are allowed on only two lakes.

Tucked into the corner of this southeastern section of the county is Lac Vieux Desert. During Lincoln's presidency this lake, which is shared with the neighboring state of Wisconsin, was included as part of a reservation and deeded to the Indians. The old village of Katakitckon and a nearby burial ground still remain on the north shore. In ancient times, Lac Vieux Desert marked the beginning of an Indian trail that led north to L'Anse and Keweenaw Bay. If you look closely while traveling US-2 about one mile west of the county line, you can see the trail where it crosses the highway.

Just outside the western edge of the Sylvania tract and also shared with Wisconsin is the Cisco Chain of Lakes. From Cisco Lake, canoeists can

paddle more than 50 miles along paths of connecting lakes that network the area.

Also included in the Ottawa National Forest on the west side of the county is the Black River Valley Recreation Area, which is of particular interest to those looking for waterfalls. In just one two-mile stretch, the main road through the area (the Black River Parkway) passes five easily accessible, beautiful waterfalls. The parkway, which parallels sections of the North Country Hiking Trail along the banks of the Black River, ends at a U.S.F.S. park with beautiful views of Black River Harbor and Lake Superior. Facilities there include a playground and a campground, and a wooden suspension bridge over the harbor leads to the sandy shores of a lovely swimming area.

In addition to the huge federal parcels, the state, too, has set aside land for public use. On the western shore of the Upper Peninsula's largest lake, for example, is a small state park with the same name as the lake — Gogebic. Hiking trails, camping, a myriad of water activities and famed walleye fishing opportunities make this park and lake a popular destination for outdoor enthusiasts. The area has earned a small but unique place in history, too. In 1889 the last stagecoach holdup east of the Mississippi took place just south of Lake Gogebic.

Other state land includes the westernmost tip of the Porcupine Mountains State Park, which projects down into Gogebic County. There, where the Presque Isle River ends its rugged path to Lake Superior, the D.N.R has developed a campground plus a network of trails that lead to beautiful waterfalls along the river's course.

Where Lake Superior graces the land with its touch, many agate beaches usually line the shore, and Gogebic County is no exception. Little Girls

Point, near the westernmost tip of the county, for example, is a good area to wander in search of the elusive stones. Little Girls Point is also fun to visit in the spring, when the area comes alive with smelt dippers.

Gogebic County is not without its manmade attractions. One particularly noticeable addition to the landscape, for example, is the "world's largest Indian," a colorful 52-foot-tall statue of Hiawatha that towers over the county's largest town, Ironwood. For an excellent view of the city, stand next to Hiawatha's moccasins and follow his steadfast and powerful gaze.

Just a few blocks away in the "Old Depot Park" in downtown Ironwood is the Ironwood Historic Museum, which is filled with information and artifacts. Iron mining was an integral part of the city's and county's early history, and there are many abandoned mines in the area.

Today the county bills itself as the "Ski Capital of the Midwest," and for good reason. The county is networked with miles of cross country ski trails, which lead from one beautiful area to another.

Downhill skiers are attracted to the four major ski areas that have been built within 14 miles of Ironwood. One, Mt. Zion, on the campus of Gogebic Community College, offers an interesting scenic lookout.

But towering above them all is the famous Copper Peak Ski Flying Hill. Sitting atop the 364-foot summit of Copper Peak, northeast of Ironwood, this 469-foot-long slide is designed to permit ski "flyers" to leap 500 feet and more. It is the only ski-flying hill in the Western Hemisphere, and the annual International Ski Flying competition attracts thousands of sports fans to the area. Many Olympians in training also use the facility to hone their phenomenal skills. During the off-season, visitors can ride an elevator to the top of the man-made structure, which juts 241 feet above the peak. From there the breathtaking view — which stretches out along the horizon to include Wisconsin, Minnesota, Canada, and the ever-present Lake Superior — is especially stunning during fall color.

Gogebic County Waterfalls Located Within the Porcupine Mountains State Park

Numerous named and unnamed waterfalls are located within the boundaries of Porcupine Mountains State Park. The walks to them range from a few feet to lengthy hikes deep into the park's interior. A small portion of the park projects into northern Ontonagon County, so descriptions of some of the area's falls are also included in that chapter.

Before you visit the Porcupine Mountains area we suggest that you first stop at the park's visitors center, just south of M-107 on South Boundary Road. There, a variety of helpful maps show the exact locations of waterfalls within the interior of the park, and park employees can provide up-to-the-minute trail conditions.

MANABEZHO FALLS

Iagoo Falls

Iagoo Falls — created as the Presque Isle River slides about six feet over a section of conglomerate rock — is more a large rapids between two smaller rapids than a falls. There is no trail to the falls, but it is close to the road and is worth the short walk through the beautiful woods.

DIRECTIONS: From M-28, just northeast of Sunday Lake in Wakefield, turn north onto CR-519 and go approximately 15 miles to Porcupine Mountains State Park. After entering the park continue on CR-519 a little less than 2 miles (to about ½ mile south of South Boundary Rd.) and park on the side of the road. The river is through the woods on the east, and though it is close to the road at this point, you should mark a trail to be safe. When you reach the river, you may have to walk slightly upstream or downstream to reach Iagoo Falls.

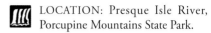 LOCATION: Presque Isle River, Porcupine Mountains State Park.

Unnamed Falls
Manabezho Falls
(Also called Presque Isle Falls)
Manido Falls
Nawadaha Falls

This is one of the most beautiful stretches of river we have found in the entire Upper Peninsula. The pristine silence of the forest here is interrupted only by the roar of water, a sound that is never far away. You can take short, easy paths from parking areas along County Road 519 to each of the falls (see DIRECTIONS) or you can follow more difficult trails along either bank of the river upstream. If you do walk the trails, use great care. The river here is wild, and signs warn of the swift current and dangerous undertows.

The riverbank route begins at the lower parking area, and a short walk leads to a network of stairs that drops to a trail. Just before the trail reaches the river, a side trail branches off to the right. Continue on the wide main path to a suspension bridge and, just above it, a fascinating unnamed falls. The unique beauty of this falls is enchanting, and the brief trip to

LOCATION: Presque Isle River, Porcupine Mountains State Park.

DIRECTIONS: From M-28, just northeast of Sunday Lake in Wakefield, turn north onto CR-519 and go approximately 15 miles to Porcupine Mountains State Park. To see the falls via the short trails from the roadway, proceed as follows: after entering the park continue on CR-519 about 3 miles to a small camper registration building on the right (about ¼ mile past the intersection with South Boundary Rd). A short walk from directly behind this building leads to Nawadaha Falls.

About ¼ mile farther on CR-519 is an

upper parking area and the start of trails to Manabezho and Manido falls. A few hundred yards farther down is the lower parking area. The path to the Unnamed Falls and the riverbank trails to the other falls begin there.

it is well worth the effort.

There, the force of the powerful river, as it rushes over its last drop before joining Lake Superior, creates miniature whirlpools along the banks. The spinning action of the water has carved perfect half-circles into the stones that line the bank and polished them to a glossy black. These arcs have also formed in the center of the river, so instead of simply falling over a shelf of rock, the water slips over the circles carved into the stone. The best views of this effect come from the bridge. The forest here draws together on both sides of the river, and branches stretch over the flow.

You could cross the bridge and take a trail along the east bank to the remaining falls, but this trail is rugged and not well groomed. We even found evidence of bear — a pine stump that had been clawed apart to expose a section of fresh wood that contrasted with the old weathered bark that once covered it.

We suggest that you retrace your steps to the side trail and follow that much easier route upstream along the west bank of the river. The narrow path leads about 200 yards through a huge section of pines, which carpet the path with needles, to Manabezho Falls. There, a thick band of white, rushing water, which spans the 150-foot-wide river, drops about 20 feet over

MANIDO FALLS

Gogebic County

a rock shelf. The largest section is tinged with gold, and its heavy flow creates a blanket of foam that trails downstream. The deep-green branches that edge the crest of the falls stretch over the water to hide the banks beneath their thick leaves.

Upstream another 100 yards, Manido Falls drops a total of about 25 feet before settling into rapids. In a mass of white water, the river descends over a network of gradually declining rock steps, then drops over a ledge of stone. From the base of the falls, the water sparkles as it slides over the rough surface of large sections of shale. The riverbanks brush up against small cliffs of rock, and beyond, the towering pines of the Porcupine Mountains are etched against the blue sky. If you look downstream, you can see the beginning of Manabezho Falls. If you look upstream past the thick woods that frame the upper portion of the falls you can see the lace curtain of Nawadaha Falls.

Nawadaha Falls is hard to see from the trail, so you may want to go down the banks to the edge of the river to get a good look at it. The rocks are so thick and the force of the flow so strong here that, as the river drops about 15 feet over a series of rock steps, it creates a blanket of white foaming lace that stretches from the top of the falls to the bottom. Maple and cedar branches extend over the river to frame this jewel of the north woods.

Shining Cloud Falls
Explorers Falls
Traders Falls
Trappers Falls

These waterfalls are located deep in the interior of the park, and if you want to visit them we suggest that you get directions and current trail conditions at the visitors center.

LOCATION: Carp River and Little Carp River, Porcupine Mountains State Park.

END OF GOGEBIC COUNTY WATERFALLS LOCATED WITHIN THE PORCUPINE MOUNTAINS STATE PARK

Lepisto Falls

 LOCATION: Presque Isle River, ½ mile south of Porcupine Mountains State Park.

As the trail to this falls leaves state park land east of CR-519, just north of the park entrance, it is gated and posted, "No Trespassing."

Nokomis Falls

 LOCATION: Presque Isle River, 2 miles south of Porcupine Mountains State Park.

We do not recommend trying to visit this falls. It is located on private property, and the trail to it is almost always blocked by a gate.

Abinodji Falls
Ogimakwe Falls
Ogima Falls

 LOCATION: Copper Creek, 2 miles south of Porcupine Mountains State Park .

We do not recommend trying to visit these three falls. All are located in a large tract of private land, and trails to them are almost always blocked by gates.

Narrows Falls

 LOCATION: Black River, 5½ miles north of Bessemer.

DIRECTIONS: From US-2 in Bessemer turn north onto CR-513 (which leads to the Black River Harbor area) and go about 6.8 miles to Narrows Spring Campground, on the right. The falls is located down the hill on the east side of the park.

The Narrows Falls is mainly a rapids, but it is tucked into a very scenic spot on a river that is popular with trout fishermen. The falls is located near the Narrows Spring Campground, and as you start down the trail from the small park you can hear the river below.

Chippewa Falls

Chippewa Falls is located in one of the most rugged settings we have visited. It is only about a quarter of a mile to the falls from the base of Copper Peak, but there is no trail and the thickly forested terrain descends steeply into a canyon. On a quiet day you can hear the waterfall from the top of the hill.

The 80-foot-wide river gradually drops about 10 feet in several sections over and around huge boulders scattered throughout the stream bed. Dead limbs and debris, which extended out from the banks overhead, were strong evidence that the river had risen much higher. Wild, thick woods — the tall, thin spires of pine etched against the azure sky — surrounds the river. Across the river the darkness of the pines encircles a small rounded meadow whose golden grasses play in the wind. Man could not create a setting as lovely as this.

LOCATION: Black River, 8 miles north of Bessemer.

DIRECTIONS: From US-2 in Bessemer turn north onto CR-513 (which leads to the Black River Harbor area) and go about 8.8 miles to a fork. Take the right fork about a mile to the Copper Peak Ski Hill area. Go just past the gift shop, then turn right and follow the road to the end of the cleared field, which is the landing zone for the ski jumpers. Head straight from the end of the landing zone down to the river. There is no marked trail, so we suggest that you mark a trail (we leave red tags and remove them on the way out) on the difficult quarter-mile walk down to the falls.

CHIPPEWA FALLS

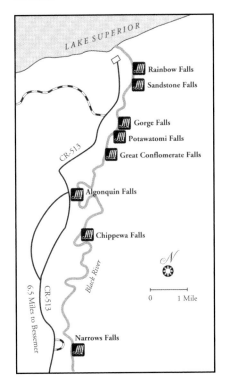

Algonquin Falls

LOCATION: Black River, 9½ miles north of Bessemer.

DIRECTIONS: From US-2 in Bessemer turn north onto CR-513 (which leads to the Black River Harbor area) and go about 8.8 miles to a fork. The right fork leads to the Copper Peak Ski Hill area then rejoins CR-513 again. Take the left fork to where the roads rejoin, then continue another 0.3 miles and park on the side of the road. Algonquin Falls is about ½ mile from the road on the right (east).

Because reliable sources had told us that Algonquin Falls is mainly a rapids, and because there are no marked trails to the falls, we chose not to visit the area. We would not recommend the hike to the inexperienced.

GREAT CONGLOMERATE FALLS

Great Conglomerate Falls
(Also known as Conglomerate Falls)
Potawatomi Falls
Gorge Falls
Sandstone Falls
Rainbow Falls

In the last few miles before County Road 513 ends at Black River Harbor, short trails — which vary from easy to steep and strenuous — lead east from the paved road through hardwood and hemlock forests to splendid views of five beautiful falls. The trail to Gorge and Potawatomi falls — because of its unusual beauty and unique design, including a series of stairways and observation platforms — has been designated a National Recreation Trail. A segment of the North Country Trail, which winds along the river in this area, also connects the falls.

At about 10.5 miles north of Bessemer the first of these trails leads three quarters of a mile to Great Conglomerate Falls. The trail is wide and smooth, but drops steadily to the riverbank.

There, the river drops in two sections around a large center chunk of conglomerate rock (which gives the falls its name) about 30 feet into a deep gorge. As the two streams descend in several quick stages, the water rushes over the angular rocks and forms small pools before plunging into the base of the gorge. The left section is bridged with logs and assorted debris that trail from the east bank to the bush-topped stone in midstream. This, plus markings on the rocks themselves, suggest that the river has been much higher. From the base, the river moves quickly downstream past heavy boulders that have fallen from the steep walls of the gorge. Farther downstream, the water rushes over these fallen rocks in a small series of rapids before disappearing behind the leafy foliage.

About a half mile farther down County Road 513 is a double-looped parking area. A very short trail from the north lot leads to Gorge Falls, and an equally brief trail from the south loop ends at Potawatomi Falls. However, we recommend that

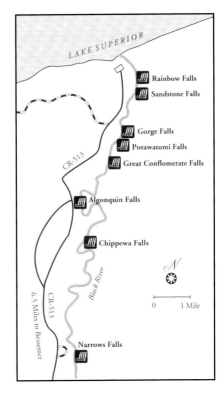

LOCATION: Black River, 10-12 miles north of Bessemer.

DIRECTIONS: From US-2 in Bessemer turn north onto CR-513 go about 13 miles to the Conglomerate Falls parking area, on the right (east). The well-marked parking areas for the other four falls are farther north along CR-513. All trails are well-marked and well-maintained by the U.S. Forest Service.

GORGE FALLS

Gogebic County

you take the trail to Potawatomi Falls, then walk along the river (following a beautiful series of fences and platforms) to Gorge Falls.

The two-minute walk along a wide path from the south parking area connects with a series of steps that drops to a trail at the river. To see Potawatomi Falls, bear right, along a wood rail fence that follows the gorge.

Potawatomi Falls is one of the most beautiful on the Black River. The falls itself is at least 40 feet high and drops in two sections around a huge mass of conglomerate stone. As the 70-foot-wide river rushes softly over the conglomerate bed, the clear water catches the sunlight, and each of the small stones interrupts the current to create thousands of sparkles.

Only the slightest bit of water covered the riverbed when we visited, but the falls was still beautiful. The water passed over the rock in small tendrils of white angel hair, which separated and joined in complicated patterns before reaching the base of the gorge. The delicate picture of this falls — nestled in the gorge and surrounded by the deep greens of high summer — is extraordinary.

Less than a quarter of a mile downstream along the fence, an extensive series of stairs rises to a viewing platform above

POTAWATOMI FALLS

and to the right of Gorge Falls. The water here flows over a mixture of conglomerate stone and smooth bedrock. At the top of the falls, the river narrows to about seven feet wide, then drops past several conglomerate boulders 20 feet into a very steep gorge. The water's pounding pressure fills the base of the falls with golden foam, which contrasts with the reddish tint of the surrounding rocks.

The river shares the path it has cut through the rock with nothing and no one. No trees cover the walls of the gorge, which are sheer and smooth and unable to hold any growth. But tall dark-green pines line the crest of the gorge, and an exquisite blanket of soft, green moss covers the rough mix of stones to near the water's edge.

About a half mile down County Road 513 from the Potawatomi/Gorge falls parking area, a quarter-mile trail — which includes a few steps roughed in with logs by the forest

SANDSTONE FALLS

Gogebic County

service — drops very steeply to Sandstone Falls. The forest is not particularly thick here, but the pines, cedars and a scattering of maples and other hardwoods tower overhead.

The falls drops in two sections. The first drop is about five feet through a network of channels the river has gouged out of the sandstone. The water then rushes between two huge conglomerate cliffs, spraying the rock to the right with a fine mist as it drops another 20 feet over a series of sandstone rocks. Upstream, you can see where the river has scooped out hollows in the conglomerate rock. Because the water level was so low, it was possible to study not only the intricate pattern the force of the water has carved into the sandstone along the banks, but also the wildflowers that grow in the tiny crevices.

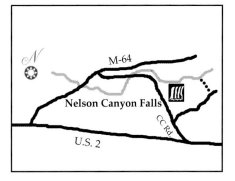

From the last parking area before the harbor, the trail to Rainbow Falls is the most strenuous. An extensive network of nearly 200 stairs descends very steeply to a platform with views of both the falls and the river upstream.

The 25-foot-wide river here narrows as it flows past huge conglomerate stones on the right. The water then rushes into a small passage between those stones and angular rock cliffs on the opposite bank, makes a sharp turn to the right, and plunges 45 feet over a mass of conglomerate rock into a black pool below. The falling water creates cascading folds of lace as it lightly drops over a huge mass of conglomerate stones in the center. The flow on the right appears to be the strongest, but because of the angle of the viewing platform it is not possible to see the far side of the falls. Foaming waves fill the pool as the force of the water pounds into its blackness. Beautiful red-gold cliffs line the darkness of the pool, and the colored rocks also edge the river as it coasts the rest of the way to Lake Superior.

Manakiki Falls

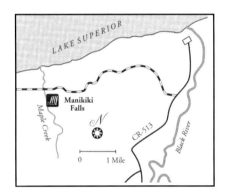

LOCATION: Maple Creek, 11 miles northeast of Bessemer.

DIRECTIONS: From US-2 in Bessemer, turn north onto CR-513 and go approximately 13.5 miles (about ½ mile past the Potawatomi/Gorge Falls parking area) to a gravel road. Turn left (west) onto this road and go approximately 3 miles to a bridge over Maple Creek.

Cross over the bridge, make a U turn and park near the bridge. The route to the falls follows the west bank of the river upstream. Although there is no trail to the falls, the quarter-mile walk to it is not too difficult.

The route to Manakiki Falls runs along the top of a ridge on the west bank of the creek about a quarter of a mile upstream to the falls. The path passes over small, rolling hills and through partially cleared woods, but across the canyon you can see a much thicker section of forest. There, dark-green pines, interspersed with mature poplar, filter the sunlight to create deep shadows over the wild land. As you approach the falls, the ridge descends to about 25 feet above the river. By the roar of the falls, the strength of the rushing river makes its presence known before you are treated to its visual impact.

As the river begins its run down through this small canyon, in a narrow slash of white water it drops quickly over a shelf of black rock, fans out to a width of three feet, then abruptly plunges through the air into a cool, clear pool 25 feet below. From the pool, the river twists right, at a 90-degree angle, and moves quietly on. Pale-brown sand lines the streambed, and the river brushes up against the sandy banks before continuing its run through the bottom of the canyon.

Saxon Falls
(Also known as Power Dam Falls)

LOCATION: Montreal River, 12 miles northwest of Ironwood.

DIRECTIONS: From Curry Park in Ironwood, go west on US-2 approximately 9.5 miles to Wisconsin County Road B. Turn right (north) onto CR-B, and go about 2.3 miles to where CR-B. turns sharply left. Continue straight ahead for ½ mile on Saxon Falls Rd. to its end. Down a hill directly opposite the road end is a power house. Saxon Falls is located just upstream from the power house.

Towering 70-foot-tall cliffs dwarf these half-hidden falls. A dam diverts about 90 percent of the water, and it is difficult to imagine what the falls might look like if normal water flow were resumed. During periods of high water, the beauty of these falls would be reborn.

Superior Falls

A tremendous drop past bordering walls of stone makes Superior Falls a beautiful spot. But like Saxon Falls, most of its water is diverted by a dam upstream, and one can't help but wonder how much more impressive it once was.

The falls alone drops 45 feet, and the total drop, including the rapids upstream, is about 75 feet. At the falls, a network of channels drops over the black rock to cover the lower section of the cliff in a wispy blanket of water before trickling into a small, dark pool below. Soft, golden cliffs rise about 100 feet above the river on the opposite bank, and bushes, which cling precariously to the stone, trail down its face in a V.

LOCATION: Montreal River, 14 miles northwest of Ironwood.

DIRECTIONS: From Curry Park in Ironwood go west on US-2 approximately 10.8 miles to Wisconsin highway 122. Turn right (north) onto W-122 and go approximatey 4.5 miles to a bridge across the Montreal River. Cross the bridge (you're back in Michigan) and turn left (west) onto the second gravel road. Follow that road to a power station, where there is a road, on the left, with a cable across it. Walk up this old road about 100 feet to the falls, on the right. The falls is located between the power station and a dam about ¼ mile upstream. Although a wood fence lines the edge of the cliffs around the viewing area, we would advise caution with children.

SUPERIOR FALLS

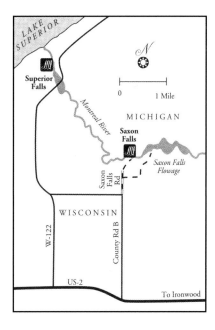

Interstate Falls
Peterson Falls

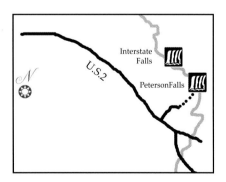 LOCATION: Montreal River, 2 miles northwest of Ironwood.

DIRECTIONS: Because the land along the Michigan side of the Montreal River is private, it is better to visit the falls from the Wisconsin side.

Go west on US-2 from Ironwood, and cross into Wisconsin. In 0.4 mile, turn right on the first road. There is a vet clinic and a small sign to Peterson Falls. Follow this road 0.3 mile to a curve to the right. There is a trail to your left from this curve which will take you to Interstate Falls. However, continue on the road for 0.1 mile to the berm at the end of the road. Park here and take the trail on the left. The 10 minute walk to Peterson Falls begins here between two large rocks. You can follow one of the many trails downstream from Peterson Falls to Interstate Falls. It is a 20 minute walk, and along the way you will pass three other falls and a long set of rapids on a small stream flowing into the river from the Michigan side. You'll appoach the falls from the top. You can return to your car by way of a trail to your left. This will take you back to the curve in the road near where you parked.

A couple of miles northwest of Ironwood, the Montreal River makes a few S-shaped curves, descends a few feet, then turns sharply to the right and plunges about 40 feet as Interstate Falls. The water drops over a scattering of rocks into a dark, moderately still pool surrounded by green trees that lean into its blackness. A wall of stone borders the falls on the left, but the remainder of the water's edge is grassy and tree-lined. From the far corner of the large, beautiful pool, the river, hidden by the leaves of the trees, continues on its way.

Upstream about a mile is Peterson Falls, which drops about 20 feet in two dramatic sections. Between these two larger falls, the river is never still on its race to the big lake, and there are several other dramatic falls as you follow the path from Interstate to Peterson.

It is thanks to the efforts of the Northwoods Land Trust that the area around Intersate Falls has been protected and is now open to the public.

INTERSTATE FALLS

Powder Horn Falls

An easy wildflower-lined footpath leads about 250 yards through thick woods to a spectacular view of a deep gorge cut out of the surroundings by Powder Mill Creek.

There, as the river shrinks to a width of only two feet, an upper falls drops about 12 feet over and around small stones that line a narrow corridor in the rock. Wedged into the length of this small chute is a fallen log, its surface wet and green with moss, and the narrow river passes inches beneath it.

The river then widens out to its original 15 feet and drops suddenly over the side of a rock wall. The powerful rush of water swoops down at least 30 feet, and the force of the river forms a beautiful pool to the right of the current. Local young people use this small pool as a summer swimming hole, but the walls of the gorge are so steep that it isn't easy to pick a path to the bottom. Where the river isn't too deep, rocks on the riverbed show through the crystal-clear water.

At the side of the falls, wildflowers have taken precarious hold in cracks in the rock, and the deep greens of pine and oak hide the sides of the gorge from summit to the pool's edge. The shadows of many branches, which bend to touch the still waters, stretch over the dark surface.

 LOCATION: Powder Mill Creek, 2 miles northwest of Bessemer.

DIRECTIONS: From US-2 near where it crosses Powder Mill Creek west of Bessemer, turn north onto Powder Horn Rd. and go about 2 miles to a supper club, on the right. (Powder Horn Rd. turns to the left at this point.) Park on the right side of the road just before the supper club, then walk back down Powder Horn Rd. to the second utility pole south of the supper club. Near this pole, you will see the well-traveled path to the falls. You will approach the falls from the top, so use caution.

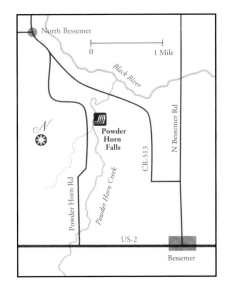

Rocky Forty Falls

Using directions from local residents, we attempted to get to this falls by walking down a set of railroad tracks, then following the stream south. But the area just south of the tracks was very swampy, and we could find no path leading upstream to the falls. We would not recommend travel to this falls.

 LOCATION: Siemens Creek, 3 miles northwest of Bessemer.

Gabbro Falls

LOCATION: Black River, 2 miles north of Ramsay.

DIRECTIONS: From the traffic signal in Wakefield go west on US-2 2.2 miles to Blackjack Rd. Turn right (north) onto Blackjack and go 1.5 miles, following it as it curves sharply left across the Black River. Just after crossing the bridge, turn left and follow the road up a hill (If you continue straight ahead you will enter a ski resort.) A short distance up the hill is a building, on the right. Make a U turn and park on the opposite side of the road. The trail begins directly across the road from the building. Because of the deep gorge, it is necessary to view the falls from above rather than at its base, so caution is advised.

A few-minutes' walk through a thick hardwood and pine forest scattered with wildflowers ends at the top of a deep gorge. There, the 10-foot-wide Black River makes a slight drop into a small pool, then suddenly plunges beyond the boulders at the edge of the cliff to fall a full 40 feet into the bottom of the gorge. Spray from the main (near) drop rises to the base of the trees at the top of the gorge, while on the far side, small wisps of water escape to run free until joining the main stream at the base of the falls. These white tendrils contrast with the black wetness of the rock, and the towering pines beyond frame the water in vibrant green.

After this striking drop, the river makes an abrupt turn to the right as it travels along the floor of the gorge. A few feet downstream, the water falls another 10 feet around a huge boulder that rests in the center of the current.

GABBRO FALLS

Neepikon Falls

Several small drops and rapids extend for hundreds of feet along this section of the Black River, about a half mile upstream from Gabbro Falls. The water was exceptionally low when we visited, which made it difficult to pinpoint exactly which of the many drops was Neepikon Falls. The rapids continue downstream for about 400 yards.

DIRECTIONS: From the traffic signal in Wakefield go west on US-2 2.2 miles to Blackjack Rd. Turn right (north) onto Blackjack and go a little less than a mile to a pumping station (Northern Natural Gas Co. Wakefield Plant) on the right (east). In a clearing across the road, follow the pipeline down to the river. Before you reach the river, the trail ends and you must go through some thick underbrush to reach the banks. The falls is located about ⅛ mile upstream from where the pipeline crosses the river.

LOCATION: Black River, 1½ miles north of Ramsay.

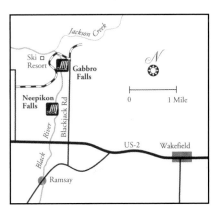

Granite Rapids Falls

Just a few feet from a parking area, the 40-foot-wide Black River quickly narrows to 15 feet as it rushes between two huge slabs of granite that reach from shore. Boulders that litter the water in midstream create a rapids as the river drops about five feet, then widens out again. Beyond a few rapids farther downstream, the river turns out of sight.

Bushes and grasses, backed by the green forest, grow right up to the banks of the river, and the shallow, crystal-clear water near the banks makes for excellent trout fishing.

DIRECTIONS: From US-2 at the traffic signal in downtown Bessemer, turn south onto Moore St. and go 0.2 miles to First St. Turn right (west) onto First and go one mile to Barber Rd. (During this mile, First will change to Spring St., then to Old County Rd.) Turn left (south) onto Barber and go 1.5 miles to Harding Rd. Turn left (east) onto Harding and go 1.5 miles to Black River Ln. Turn right (south) onto Black River Ln. and go 0.9 miles to the end of the road. The rapids are on the left.

LOCATION: Black River, 3 miles southeast of Bessemer.

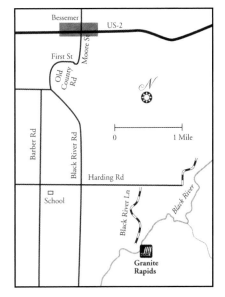

Yondota Falls

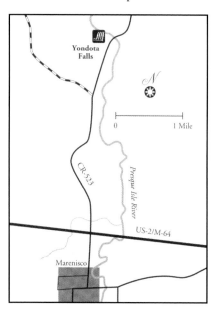

LOCATION: Presque Isle River, 4 miles north of Marenisco.

DIRECTIONS: From US-2/M-64 just west of the Presque Isle River near Marenisco, turn north onto CR-523 and go 3 miles to a bridge that crosses the Presque Isle River. Cross the bridge, make a U turn and park near a sign, on the west side of the road, that marks the start of the trail to the falls.

A small path on the right bank leads downstream, through thick woods and past wildflowers, to a log archway. Continue beneath the wood arch about 50 feet to the trail's end at the top of the falls.

A five-minute walk along a short, easy trail ends at the top of Yondota Falls.

The Presque Isle River is close to 30 feet wide here, but it narrows to five feet as it drops about eight feet in a rush through a very narrow gorge that has been carved out of the dark rock. To the right of this small channel, unusual pink traces of color decorate the dark surface of a huge slab of bedrock. Lines, which also mark its surface, suggest that the water level has once risen to cover this rock.

At the end of the chute of water, the river widens, then falls in three sections over and around more of the huge, pink-tinged, dark boulders. These rocks, which divide the force of the water as it runs past them, are large and dry enough to walk on.

YONDOTA FALLS

Little Giant Falls

LOCATION: Little Giant Creek, 3 miles north of Marenisco

Though this falls is included on most waterfall lists, we could find no one in the area who had ever heard of it.

Judson Falls
(Also known as Slate River Falls)

Nelson Canyon Falls
(Also known as Marshalls Falls)

Though both of these falls are located fairly close to main roads, rangers at Lake Gogebic State Park told us that many people have become lost searching for them. We are including directions to Nelson Canyon Falls, but if you want to visit Judson Falls, we recommend you talk to park rangers before attempting the hike.

The trail to Nelson Canyon Falls takes visitors through a deeply shaded hardwood forest, and as you approach the falls, it makes an abrupt 15 foot drop over the dark angled stone. Upstream, a tumble of black boulders forces the river to zig zag down to the falls.

LOCATION: Slate River, 1 mile south of Lake Gogebic and Nelson Creek, 1½ miles south of Lake Gogebic.

DIRECTIONS: Turn north on M-64 from US-2. Continue for 2.4 miles, turning right on Camp C Rd. Continue for 1.2 miles to a two-track on the left. This is just past the second culvert you will see. You could drive up the small hill to enter the two track and follow it to its end a it fades out to the right. Because of very wet conditions, we chose to park on the main road and walk to the end of the two-track, about ¼ mile. From here, it is about 200 yards on your left to the river. Mark your trail in with ribbons. Follow the river downstream a little less than a mile to the falls.

Kakabika Falls

An easy-to-follow trail leads 200 yards through the woods to the base of this beautiful, secluded falls.

There, in a 100-yard-long series of drops over shiny black stone, the 20-foot-wide river swiftly descends 40-50 feet. A 3-foot-wide gorge, worn into the stone by the current, guides the river down the last drop. Thick, green moss cushions and colors the black rocks, which extend above the water line, and also covers the rock cliffs that rise up from both sides of the river.

Like most streams in this area, the water is copper-colored. Several fallen trees span the river, and the swift flow has also left countless logs and branches washed up against the banks.

DIRECTIONS: From US-2 approximately 16 miles west of Watersmeet or 12.5 miles east of Marenisco, turn north onto CR-527 (marked with a sign) and go about ½ mile to a one-lane bridge over the Ontonagon River. Do not cross the bridge, but rather, park on the left side of the road (a sign marks the falls) and follow the trail downstream. Wildflowers and bushes line the beginning of the trail, but then the forest becomes quite thick and fills the air with an ever-present scent of cedar.

LOCATION: Cisco Branch Ontonagon River, 2½ miles southeast of Gogebic Station.

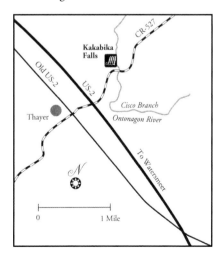

Ajibikoka Falls

 LOCATION: Brush Lake, 5 miles northwest of Watersmeet.

Though this falls is located on public land north of County Road 206 in an area near the north end of Brush Lake, there are no marked trails to it. Therefore, we would not recommend visiting this falls.

Mex-i-min-e Falls
(Also known as Burned Dam Falls)

 LOCATION: Middle Branch Ontonagon River, 6½ miles northeast of Watersmeet.

DIRECTIONS: From US-45 in Watersmeet turn east onto Old US-2, also called CR-208, and go about 6.2 miles to a gravel road marked by a "Burned Dam Campgrounds" sign. Turn left (north) onto this unnamed road (called USFS-169 on U.S. Forest Service maps) and go 1.1 miles to the entrance to Burned Dam Campground. Turn left into the campground. The trail to the falls is on the left as you enter.

The easy-to-follow dirt trail leads through a predominantly pine forest about 100 feet to the base of the falls.

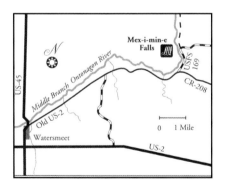

During the lumbering heyday in the late 1800s, a dam was built on top of this falls. Logs were held behind the dam until spring, when the gates were opened allowing logs and water to rush to the town of Interior, which had sprung up about six miles downstream. But around 1900 a forest fire destroyed both the town and the dam (the reason for the falls' second name). Today, a sign and a graveyard are all that's left of Interior, and only huge cracked boulders line the edges of the river.

At the falls the swift flow splashes against those rocks as the 40-foot-wide river drops a total of about 15 feet. First are a few small drops, then the water slides over huge slabs of gently sloping black rock for a total descent of about five feet. Directly downstream, the river rushes over the flat, slightly angled black stone to its largest drop, perhaps seven feet, past both sides of a huge dry-topped boulder in midstream. Beyond this drop, the falls ends in a rush of white water that splashes over small rocks and stones.

Iron County

Iron County's roots reach deep into the iron and lumber industry of the 1800s. The county's mines ran the length of the western section of the Menominee Iron Range, and Crystal Falls was the headquarters of mining in that area.

Of special significance to the lumbering industry is the fact that Iron County is a part of a huge watershed that eventually runs into the Menominee River, a 180-mile-long flow that forms the Upper Peninsula's southern border from the southeast corner of Iron County to Lake Michigan. The Michigamme, the Paint, the Brule, and several other rivers that extend their network of streams and tributaries into the Menominee formed a perfect path for lumbermen to float their logs to the mills.

Today, this river system is renowned for its fishing, and many anglers try their luck along it and the county's other countless miles of rivers and streams. Lakes, too, abound in Iron County. On the shores of one, First Fortune Lake, is Bewabic State Park, which is an excellent site for water recreation and fishing.

The Iron County Museum, in Caspian, is an excellent place to become more acquainted with the distinctive traits of Iron County, and its unique and enjoyable collection of artifacts from bygone days is well worth a visit. More than 50 major exhibits, dozens of smaller exhibits, and 13 buildings add up to a full afternoon's excursion, especially for those interested in the mining and lumber industries. Included in the museum park are homes of the county's early pioneers as well as displays of pioneer life during the early chapters of the county's history.

Snake Rapids

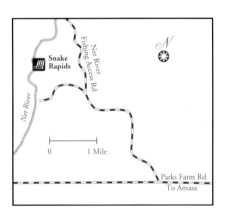

LOCATION: Net River, 8 miles west of Amasa.

DIRECTIONS: From US-141 just south of Amasa, turn west onto Parks Farm Rd. (called West Pine St. on the east side of US-141) and go 3.3 miles to a fork. Take the right (north) fork and follow the public access signs about 2.5 miles to another fork. Take the left fork and continue to follow the public-access signs about 1.4 miles to a campground at the river. The rapids are about ¼ mile upstream.

West of Amasa, the 50-foot-wide Net River narrows to form Snake Rapids. At the base of the quarter-mile-long rapids, the river widens out again to a near lake-size 200 feet. There, towering pines on the far shore are reflected in the clear, copper-tinged water. Angling opportunities promise to be excellent, and the shallow rapids make them an ideal spot for fishermen with waders. Facilities at a state-forest campground near the base of the rapids include several secluded campsites, pit toilets and a boat ramp.

The trail to the rapids involves a five-minute walk along an overgrown and long-forgotten dirt road to the river. From there the trail follows the riverbank upstream about a quarter of a mile. Heavy underbrush surrounds the riverbank path, and the air is thick with the enticing smell of the large cedars that line the route. Here and there, wildflowers poke through the fresh green ferns that carpet the forest floor.

Chipmunk Falls

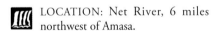

LOCATION: Net River, 6 miles northwest of Amasa.

The land on both sides of the river at the falls is privately owned.

Margeson Falls

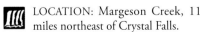

LOCATION: Margeson Creek, 11 miles northeast of Crystal Falls.

Though this falls is located on state land, all access roads that we found were on posted private property.

Iron County

Lower Hemlock Rapids
Hemlock Rapids

Routes to both rapids cross private property, so we were unable to reach them.

 LOCATION: Paint River, 3 miles southwest of Amasa.

Chicagon Falls

The best views of this falls come from an easily accessible small island.

To get to it you must navigate the twists and turns of a trail that passes through a thickly wooded oak, birch and poplar forest. Wildflowers and blackberry brambles cover the ground, and as the trail nears the falls, you can smell the huge cedars that line the river. The trail breaks out of the forest at the top of the falls, where a little stream jogs to the right around a small island. The trail crosses this stream to the island and views of the falls from its head.

The 25-foot-wide river drops about three feet, then turns to the left and swiftly slides 20 feet down a flat chute of rock. After foaming over huge black boulders in the middle of the current, the river falls again, about five feet, then settles down to skate over rocks and cedar roots as it widens out farther downstream.

DIRECTIONS: Go to Bewabic State Park on US-2 for directions to the falls. This will avoid problems with crossing private property.

LOCATION: Chicagon Creek, 6 miles northwest of Crystal Falls.

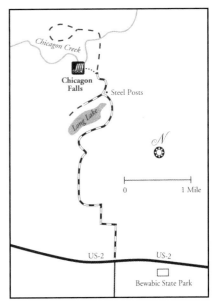

Glidden Rapids

DIRECTIONS: Go east of Crystal Falls on M-69 about 5.2 miles to the Michigamme River. Cross the river and park on the right (south) side of M-69. To reach the rapids walk ½ mile downstream on the east bank. The first 100 yards is through a low-lying swampy area, but after crossing a few small creeks, the terrain climbs steeply to the top of a hill. Continue walking along this hill for 15 minutes and the rapids will be around the first bend in the river after the hill..

There is no trail to this small rapids, which drop only about a foot, and the route to them requires a rough 20-minute trek through the forest. During normal or high-water conditions, the river would probably swallow up this rapids. We visited during a dry spring, when the river was low, and that is probably the only reason they were visible.

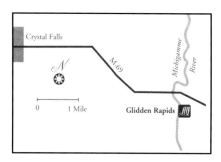

Horserace Rapids

LOCATION: Paint River, 8 miles southeast of Crystal Falls.

DIRECTIONS: Go approximately 7 miles south of Crystal Falls on US-2/US-141 to Horserace Rapids Rd., just before the Joseph Caspary Roadside Park. (A sign just before this intersection points to the Iron County Airport and Horserace Rapids Rd.) Turn left (east) onto the blacktopped road and go 1.7 miles to the junction with Airport Rd. Turn right (south) and continue on Horserace Rapids Rd 0.7 miles to the Horserace Rapids parking area.

Once, according to local legend, a lumberman either deliberately or accidentally rode a log down the length of Horserace Rapids. The Paint River was used to float logs to the mills, and as the man worked to break up a log jam, as the story goes, it broke loose and he was carried along with it. Tales like that, plus spectacular natural beauty, make Horserace Rapids a very appealing stop. The road to the falls ends on a bluff, and a short walk down the steep rock-strewn hillside ends at a scattering of huge pines and cedars that reach high above the river.

But an 80-foot-high bluff on the opposite side of the river towers over even those majestic trees and fills the sky with its dark presence. One of the most striking features of this bluff is an unusual almost aqua-colored moss that is scattered

HORSERACE RAPIDS

over its surface. This light aqua-green mixes with the darker greens and browns of the forest to create a beautiful display of changing hues.

In the river below, Horserace Rapids rushes over huge, sharp rocks that have tumbled from the banks. The rapids stretch for hundreds of yards down the 30-foot-wide river. When we visited, the water level was lower than usual, but in the past it has been high enough to float logs.

Not far away, on the Menominee River in Dickinson County, is another Horserace Rapids. That falls, the first to be named, has been swallowed up by the backwaters of the Hydraulic Falls Dam.

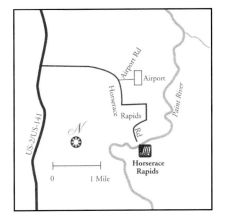

Iron County Dam Sites

Little Bull Falls Dam

LOCATION: Paint River, 6 miles southeast of Crystal Falls.

DIRECTIONS: Go about 5 miles east of Crystal Falls on M-69 to Lake Mary Rd. Turn right (south) onto Lake Mary Rd. and go 3.6 miles to Little Bull Rd. Turn right (west) onto Little Bull and go one mile to a fork. Take the right fork one mile to the dam site.

There is no waterfall remaining at this site, which is called Public Recreation Area #22.

Brule Island Falls Dam

LOCATION: Brule River, 11½ miles southeast of Crystal Falls.

There are no waterfalls at this dam site, which is surrounded by private property. This site may be reached by going north on Chapin Street out of Florence, Wisconsin.

Michigamme Falls Dam
(Also known as Lower Michigamme Falls)

LOCATION: Michigamme River, 10 miles southeast of Crystal Falls

DIRECTIONS: Go east out of Crystal Falls on M-69 about 5.2 miles to the Michigamme River. Cross the river and continue east another 4.5 miles to Camp 5 Rd. Turn right (south) onto Camp Five Rd. and go approximately 9.7 miles to Lower Dam Rd. Turn right (west) onto Lower Dam Rd. and go 2.7 miles to the dam site.

There is no waterfall remaining at this site, which is called Recreation Area #8. Facilities there include a boat ramp and pit toilets.

Peavy Falls Dam
(Also known as Upper Michigamme Falls)

LOCATION: Michigamme River, 9 miles southeast of Crystal Falls.

DIRECTIONS: Go east out of Crystal Falls on M-69 about 5.2 miles to the Michigamme River. Cross the river and continue east on M-95 another 4.5 miles to Camp 5 Road and go approximately 7 miles to Upper Dam Rd. Turn right (west) onto Upper Dam Rd. and go 2.4 miles to the dam site.

There is no waterfall remaining at this site, which is called Public Recreation Site #9.

Hemlock Falls Dam

There is no waterfall remaining at the site of the dam.

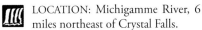 LOCATION: Michigamme River, 6 miles northeast of Crystal Falls.

DIRECTIONS: Go 4.2 miles east of Crystal Falls on M-69 to a blacktop road. (A sign just before the intersection reads, "Mansfield Location."). Turn left (north) onto the unnamed road and go about 2.5 miles (after 1.5 miles the road becomes Old M-69 Rd.) to where it turns to the right and meets the Michigamme River. Do not cross the river, but rather turn left at a sign that commemorates the Mansfield Mine disaster (many miners were killed when the Michigamme River broke into the mine) and go 1.5 miles to the dam site.

The mouth of Craigs Mine hides in the deep shadows of the forest, abandoned for decades. The upper peninsula is dotted with deserted gold, silver, copper and iron ore mines, much like this one in Marquette County. Craigs Mine, a gold mine, is a good example of the typical adit mine; miners dug a nearly horizontal tunnel into the hill, making it easier for the ore to be hauled out.

Dickinson, Menominee and Delta Counties

Bordered by Wisconsin on the west and the beautiful Green Bay of Lake Michigan on the east, Delta, Menominee and Dickinson counties form the southernmost tip of the Upper Peninsula. Because of the small number of waterfalls in each of these counties, we've combined them into one chapter.

As in the rest of the U.P., countless outdoor pursuits are available in this tri-county area. Thousands of acres have been set aside for public enjoyment in the Hiawatha National Forest and the Copper Country, Escanaba River, and Lake Superior state forests. Their many lakes, streams and forests have been visited by generations of serious hunters and fishermen.

One of the most popular and beautiful rivers in the area is the Menominee, which winds its way along the western border of Dickinson and Menominee counties to form the Michigan/Wisconsin state line. Thick woods and steep, rocky cliffs surround the wide, swiftly flowing river. The Menominee, once famous for the abundant whitefish and sturgeon in its deep-blue waters, now offers good walleye fishing opportunities, especially in the backwaters of its dams.

In Menominee County long before roads were built, the extensive river system served as the main mode of travel throughout the area. Those who used the waters left a rich historical heritage, and it is easy to fill several days investigating this county's past. Ancient Native Americans used the waterway to travel to the copper pits in the Keweenaw Peninsula and on Isle Royale. The southern portion of the river was home to the Menominee Indians, who played a large part in

the area's history. As Europeans spread throughout the area, the river was used to remove timber harvests and as a route in the search for fortunes in minerals hidden beneath the earth.

One of those minerals, iron ore, has also played an important role in the history of Dickinson County. The Eastern Menominee Iron Range stretches through the county, and several abandoned mine sites in the area that are open to the public provide a fascinating glimpse into the past. One of the most interesting remnants of the mining era is the Cornish Pumping Engine, the largest steam engine ever built in North America. The 50-foot-high pump, which may be visited in Iron Mountain, was used to remove water from the Chapin Mine, the area's most productive iron mine. Another landmark in Dickinson County is the Pine Mountain Ski Jump, near Iron Mountain. Well-known for its annual mid-February tournaments, Pine Mountain is, at 932 feet, the longest ski jump in the world.

Bordering Lake Michigan northeast of Menominee County is Delta County, whose highways are major crossroads for Upper Peninsula travelers. The proximity to Lake Michigan originally opened up the county to industrial interests, and its largest city, the port of Escanaba, is still a major shipping point for iron ore from mines to the north. The city is also the permanent site of the Upper Peninsula State Fair, which is held annually in August.

Directly east of Escanaba, across both Little and Big Bay De Noc, is one of Michigan's most fascinating ghost towns. Located on the west side of the aptly named Garden Peninsula, which juts into Lake Michigan to help form Big Bay De Noc, the town of Fayette was originally established in 1867 by Fayette Brown as the site of a smelting operation for the Jackson Iron Company. But the area's hardwoods, which are needed for the smelting process, gradually were depleted, and in 1891, after producing nearly 230,000 tons of pig-iron, the company abandoned Fayette.

During the 1960s the State of Michigan purchased the area and turned it into one of our most beautiful state parks. The town is situated on the shores of Snail Shell Harbor, a beautiful natural cove formed by a high limestone bluff to its north and a small strip of land to its south. Pretty and unusual stones cover the shoreline, which makes the walk to a campground south of the townsite especially beautiful. Several of the original buildings have been restored, complete with furnishings of the period, and parts of the old kilns and the main smelting building are still standing. An informative interpretive center has been added. It's easy to spend many hours here,

and as you walk through the once-bustling town, you can't escape the eerie sensation that it is in a state of suspended animation, just waiting for an opportunity to come alive again.

Another natural attraction in the area that you won't want to miss is Kitch-iti-ki-pi (Big Spring), located in Palms Book State Park in Schoolcraft County. This 300-foot-long, 75-foot-wide, 40-foot-deep elliptical pond is Michigan's largest spring, and it is beautiful. The best way to enjoy it is by taking a self-propelled raft across the water, which is as clear as glass. As you glide quietly over the pond, through a hole in the center of the raft you can see trees laying silently on the sandy bottom, the tendrils of the moss that covers them drifting slowly back and forth in the current. If you look closely, you can even see huge rainbow trout that hide beneath the fallen logs. And at the very bottom of the bowl, if the light is just right, it is possible to catch a glimpse of the sand that billows out in small puffs from the action of the spring beneath the earth's surface.

Mill Pond Falls

LOCATION: Sundholm Creek, one mile southwest of Felch.

Though the falls is located just south of the Swedish Lutheran Church, about one mile southwest of Felch, it cannot be reached from there without crossing private property. The approach from the southeast involves a compass- and map-guided trek across state land. We would not advise visiting this falls without first obtaining directions from the D.N.R. Field Office in Felch.

Horserace Rapids

LOCATION: Menominee River, one mile south of East Kingsford.

Horserace Rapids is located in the backwaters of Hydraulic Dam, and is visible only during periods of low water. During two visits to this area, we saw no sign of a rapids.

Little Quinnesec Falls
(Also known as Kimberly Clark Falls)

LOCATION: Menominee River, 4 miles southwest of Norway.

The land on the Michigan side of this falls is privately owned, and there are no good views from the Wisconsin side. From the Kimberly Clark plant, which stretches along the river in Niagara, Wisconsin, it is possible to get a partial view of the falls as it runs over the black rocks near the right edge of the factory.

DIRECTIONS: Go south from Norway on US-8 and cross the Menominee River into Wisconsin. Continue on US-8 for approximately 3 more miles as it bears west to US-141. Turn right (north) onto US-141 and go about 3 miles to the town of Niagara. As you drive through Niagara, you will see the Menominee River, about a block away on the right. Drive down any of the streets that lead to the street that follows next to the river, turn left and go until you see the large paper mill on the right. Park in a large truck lot, on the right just before reaching the mill. The falls is upstream about 400 yards, but there is no access across the private property.

Fumee Falls

On the north edge of the Helen Z. Lien Roadside Park, Fumee Creek makes a few drops, forms a small pool, then falls 25 feet over the side of a limestone bluff, which looms out from towering cedars and pines. As the water falls it forms two small streams, which glide over and around dark, moss-covered rocks. These stones are particularly interesting because, unlike the smooth, softly rounded stones found at most waterfalls, they have yet to succumb to the water's persistent erosion and are sharply angled and rough-surfaced.

From the base of the falls, fallen rocks stretch down a hill to a small footbridge, which spans the 5-foot-wide creek. You can glimpse this falls from your car, and a short walk will take you to the water's edge. A small, short trail leads to the top of the bluff.

LOCATION: Fumee Creek, 3½ miles northwest of Norway.

DIRECTIONS: Go almost 4 miles west of Norway on US-2 to the Helen Z. Lien Roadside Park, on the north side of the highway.

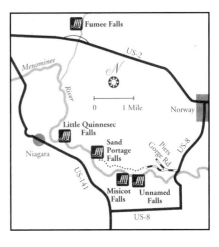

FUMEE FALLS

Unnamed Falls
Misicot Falls
Sand Portage Falls

LOCATION: Menominee River, 3 miles southwest of Norway.

DIRECTIONS: From Norway go south on US-8 about 1½ miles to Piers Gorge Rd., which is the last road before crossing the Menominee River. Turn right (west) onto Piers Gorge Rd. and go about ½ mile to a fork. Take the left fork and follow the gravel road one mile to the parking area and the start of the trail.

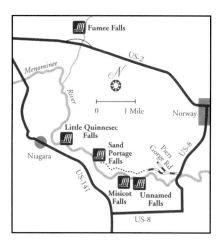

In the Piers Gorge Scenic Area, just south of Norway, the beautiful Menominee River drops four times. Not all of these falls are named or shown on maps, but they can be easily seen by following a smooth, clear trail through the hardwood forest. This area once was referred to as the Great Sand Portage, because Indians used to carry their canoes from the base of the unnamed falls to the upper end of Sand Portage Falls. Legend has it that the variegated rock, which composes most of the trail, has been worn smooth by the countless moccasins that have tread the ground during those portages.

The trail begins by crossing through a cedar swamp, so common to the U.P., and as it passes beneath the fragrant boughs, it crosses two foot bridges. Just after crossing the second bridge, through the trees on the left is an unnamed falls, which drops about a foot in a golden band of color across the entire river.

From there the trail climbs over a few stones and roots up the face of a rock hill, but the path is still easy. From the crest of the hill, crowned with huge oaks and pines, you can see the river clearly. On the left is the second falls which, similar to the first, is more like a rapids, with short drops continuing for several feet.

The trail continues down to the right, and when we visited in May, a riot of trillium formed a snowy backdrop to the deep browns and greens of the forest. The trail descends through the towering trees back to the river and, on the left, Misicot Falls. The trail is still about 70 feet above the water, and the view is encompassing.

Past the treetops you can see the swift, dangerous current as it rushes across the rocks, then foams over the 5-foot drop of the main falls. The 150-foot-wide river narrows drastically as it passes over the falls, and the black water rolls up toward the sky as it sweeps over a large boulder in the middle of the flow. The river then continues in a cascade of small rapids.

Just downstream from the falls, you can see that this area is aptly named. There, the strength of the Menominee River has cut through the rock to form a 60-foot-deep gorge. The walls of this gorge jut out from the shore just past the falls, and as the river curves around the steep rock face, the stone

MISICOT FALLS

wall takes the full force of the water. Eventually it, too, will wear away.

The trail continues upstream and, about 30 minutes from Misicot Falls, passes beneath a power line. Take the next trail to the left, and as you turn through the woods you can hear Sand Portage Falls. The short walk ends at the edge of a 30-foot-high cliff with excellent views of the river and the falls. The river splits around a small island, and as it narrows where the two flows rejoin, Sand Portage Falls begins. Similar to both unnamed falls, this is more like a rapids, but it has a larger and longer drop than either of the unnamed falls.

The Piers Gorge Scenic Area was one of the loveliest in this part of the state in terms of the nature and wildlife it afforded. During our early morning visit, we saw several ducks, frogs and dozens of deer tracks. Silver squirrels ran through the leaves, a walleye was pulled from the waters, and we heard the haunting call of Canadian geese as they flew swiftly up the river, following its every turn.

Dickinson County Dam Sites

Twin Falls Dam

LOCATION: Menominee River.

There is no waterfall at this site, located near Iron Mountain about four miles north of US-2 on CR-607.

Ford Falls Dam

LOCATION: Menominee River.

There is no waterfall at this site, located near Kingsford on Cowboy Lake Road, off Woodward Avenue.

Hydraulic Falls Dam
(Also known as Big Quinnesec Falls)

LOCATION: Menominee River.
DIRECTIONS: From US-141 in East Kingsford turn west onto Brietung Rd. and go one mile to Hydraulic Falls Dam Rd. Turn left (south) onto that road and go 0.3 miles to the dam.

There is no visible waterfall at this site.

Sturgeon Falls Dam

LOCATION: Menominee River.
DIRECTIONS: From CR-577 about 2.5 miles south of Vulcan, turn west onto Power Dam Rd. and go about 1/2 mile to the dam.

Water spills over a small section of the dam, but there is no natural waterfall at this site.

Power Dam Falls

LOCATION: Sturgeon River.
DIRECTIONS: Go north out of Loretto on CR-573 and turn right (east) onto the first gravel road. Continue east to the second gravel road on the left. Turn left (north) and follow this road to the dam.

There is no waterfall at this site.

Quiver Falls

Because the Michigan side is private property, Quiver Falls must be viewed from the Wisconsin banks of the Menominee River.

A small island divides the river here, and a set of rapids flows 200-300 yards on each side of it before joining again. The bigger drop is on the Wisconsin side. The water also swirls softly around log pilings, which stretch up from the river as an eerie reminder of what once must have been an old wooden dam or railroad bridge.

DIRECTIONS: Cross over the Menominee River south of Norway on US-8 into Wisconsin and go about 3 miles to US-141. Turn left (south) onto US-141 and go about 8.5 miles to Kremlin Rd. Turn left (east) onto Kremlin and go about 9 miles to the uninhabited village of Kremlin. From the intersection of three roads in Kremlin, continue straight and cross a set of railroad tracks. Just after crossing the tracks, the road forks. Take the left fork (the right fork is blocked by a large sand bank) and follow it about a mile as it winds to a parking area near the river. A short trail from the parking area leads to the river, and the falls is about ¼ mile upstream.

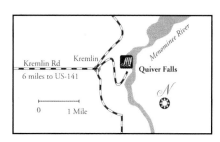

LOCATION: Menominee River, 3½ miles southwest of Faithorn.

Pemene Falls

Down some steps only about 70 feet from a parking area is uniquely beautiful Pemene Falls. The falls is more like a rapids as the river drops about seven feet in a 100-yard strip. The thick forest here spreads toward the edge of the river but is halted by sheets of rough, black rocks, which gradually creep from under the surface of the water, then angle sharply upward to pave the banks. The rock is slippery even above the water, evidence that the river level fluctuates. A few cement abutments indicate that the area may once have been dammed.

DIRECTIONS: From Faithorn go south about 8.5 miles on CR-577 to CR-374. Turn right (west) onto CR-374. and go about 3 miles to the last sand road before crossing a bridge over the Menominee River. (Just before this intersection is a D.N.R. public-access sign on the right.) Turn right (north) onto the sand road and go ½ mile to the Jerry Welling Site.

From there, you can see the falls upstream, but to reach them you must continue north about another ½ mile to a trail road that heads left into the woods. That trail leads 0.1 mile to the parking lot area at the falls.

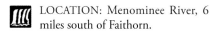

LOCATION: Menominee River, 6 miles south of Faithorn.

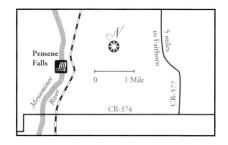

Chandler Falls

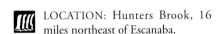 LOCATION: Unnamed Stream, 6 miles north of Escanaba.

We were informed by D.N.R. officials in Escanaba that, because of a dam, this falls, located about two miles southeast of Carrel Corners, is under water and no longer visible.

Hunters Brook Falls

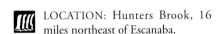 LOCATION: Hunters Brook, 16 miles northeast of Escanaba.

This falls — which, according to local residents, is located near where Hunters Brook empties into the Escanaba River — is on private property.

Rapid River Falls

LOCATION: Rapid River, 7 miles north of Rapid River.

Because of its easy access in a large, grassy park, Rapid River Falls is a popular stopping place.

The river is about 40 feet wide, and the falls spans it as a copper-tinted ribbon of water. Four tiers, spread several feet apart, drop a total of 12 feet before the river rushes past the park on its left bank. Smooth limestone slabs, similar to those at Whitefish Falls (see page 26), border the banks to make a smooth, easy trail. The river rushes swiftly between the stone borders, which hold back the trees somewhat.

All in all, this is a very pleasant park to enjoy a family picnic or just to stop for a few minutes and visit the falls. Children, too, will enjoy the playground and the river nearby. Facilities at the large park include picnic tables, barbeque pits and a flowing well.

DIRECTIONS: Go 6.5 miles north of Rapid River on US-41 to S-15 Road, the last road before crossing the Rapid River. Turn left (west) onto S-15 and go 0.3 mile to the park and falls.

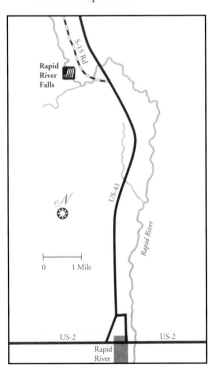

Delta County

Haymeadow Falls

The walk to Haymeadow Falls is a lovely 10-minute trip along a marked trail through a thick hardwood forest, over rolling hills and past tiny streams to Haymeadow Creek.

There, in a copper-colored band, the 15-foot-wide falls drops about three feet, then foams up over fallen rocks at its base before continuing down the river. A lush cedar and birch forest touches the riverbanks, and a fallen tree spans the creek below the falls. A bridge, which crosses the stream at the base of the falls, is a perfect spot for picture-taking.

In the back of our minds as we traveled through the backwoods of northern Michigan, we always hoped for a glimpse of large animals, such as deer or perhaps even a rare bear. Near the bottom of our mental wildlife list were smaller animals.

But that changed at Haymeadow Falls. As we gazed at the falls, we saw a splash of water followed by a silver, glistening object that hurled itself from the base of the falls. A salmon had tried to leap the falls. It brought to mind the wonders that had gone unseen beneath the flows and drops we had visited. We see only the beauty of the falls and the peaceful drifting of the river, but the beauty continues below the surface and is there for all who would care to notice.

 LOCATION: Haymeadow Creek, 9 miles northeast of Rapid River.

DIRECTIONS: From the blinker light on the east side of Rapid River, go about 2 miles east on US-2 to where it bears south at CR-509. Continue straight (east) on CR-509, go about ½ mile, and turn left (the road is still CR-509). Go north on CR-509 about 8 miles to a fork. The paved right fork is 33rd Rd. (also called CR-442). Take the gravel left fork, which is CR-509, about ⅛ mile to Haymeadow Campground, marked with a sign on the right. The trail to the falls begins at the northeast corner of the campgrounds. About 150 feet after you start down the old four-wheel-drive trail, a walking trail branches left to the falls. Although this path is marked by a small sign, it is very easy to miss.

A second trail to the falls begins at a parking area, on the right about ¼ mile past the campgrounds on CR-509.

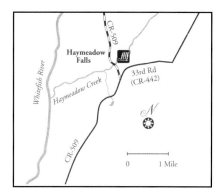

Delta County Dam Sites

Boney Falls Dam

DIRECTIONS: Go 7 miles north of Cornell on CR-523 to a set of limestone pillars on the right and a sign that reads, "Escanaba Power Dam #4 Boney Falls." This is the entrance to the dam.

 LOCATION: Escanaba River.

Lower Peninsula Waterfalls

Ocqueoc Falls

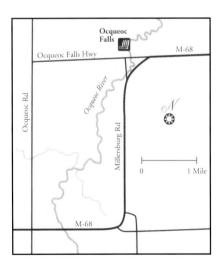

LOCATION: Ocqueoc River, 9 miles east of Onaway.

DIRECTIONS: Go approximately 6 miles east of Onaway on M-68 to Ocqueoc Rd. Turn left (north) onto Ocqueoc and go about 2.8 miles to Ocqueoc Falls Hwy. Turn right (east) onto Ocqueoc Falls Hwy. and go approximately 1.5 miles to the Ocqueoc River. Cross the river and turn left, into the parking area. The paved trail to the falls heads west, through a small picnic area, about 100 feet to the falls. There is also a smooth wooden ramp that will bypass the stairs and take you directly to the river's edge.

As the Lower Peninsula's only named waterfall, Ocqueoc Falls certainly deserves to be included in this collection. Located in a secluded section of woodland, this falls is a beautiful addition to any trip to the area, and its charm shouldn't be missed.

Less than 100 feet from a parking area, the Ocqueoc River makes three drops for a total of about 10 feet. As the water sweeps over the smooth shelves of black rock, the falls forms snow-white accents between each level section of the river.

A mixture of hardwoods surrounds the falls, and a few dark-green pines are scattered along the banks. As you walk through a thick layer of dried oak leaves, which have covered the earth since the previous autumn, the only sounds that pierce the silence are the leaves rustling underfoot and the muted roar of the river hidden beyond the trees. As you approach the river, the trails of light-brown leaves dwindle, and a few fall into the rushing water.

OCQUEOC FALLS

Index of Waterfalls

Many waterfalls in this book have been known or are presently known by more than one name. Following is a listing of all the known names of every waterfall and dam site in the book.

166

Waterfalls that may be viewed from a car